30 WAYS IN 30 DAYS
TO A BETTER LIFE

STEVE MELIA

30 WAYS IN 30 DAYS
TO A BETTER LIFE

ISBN: 978-0-9892123-2-8
Printed in the United States of America

To order, go to:
www.the162crew.com

Acknowledgments

Thanks to everyone who has been part of my journey.

Mike: Thanks for being my partner for the last 25 years. I'll always appreciate you and all that you have done for me. Thanks for your continued support.

Marybeth Longona: Thank you for your help in accomplishing 30 Ways in 30 Days. Your daily pep talks, feedback and creative ideas helped me push through and get this done. Your love and encouragement have been amazing and I could not have done it without you.

To Mary, Steve, and Matt: Thanks for being a huge part of my life and for your continued encouragement.

Tommy and Lucy: Thank you for always being there; you define what being family is all about.

Danny (Godfather) and Maureen: I'll always be grateful for your love and support.

Eileen (Godmother) and Michael: Thanks for always being there and supporting me and my crazy ideas.

To all of my nieces and nephews, I am one lucky uncle to the most amazing people in the world. Keep living your dreams.

Macie Grace and the Bryant family: I'm so grateful for being part of your lives. You make me smile every day.

Kim: Thanks for your partnership and friendship. I look forward to another 20 years of making money and helping people.

To Jeff Bell: Thanks for coming into my life in 2014 and reigniting my passion for success. Your leadership is inspiring.

Brian Carruthers: Thanks for always staying true to who you are and being a great example for the rest of us.

Kelsey Aida Roualdes: Thank you for being part of this book and sharing your love and light with the world.

To all of my friends at LegalShield: Thanks for giving me the opportunity of a lifetime and your unwavering support.

Thanks to all of our Hogar Heros who continue to support Work, Play, Love every month.

To all my Yankee friends: Thanks for making the journey so much fun!

To Brian Mast: Thank you for helping me put this book together. Your professionalism and guidance certainly made this book possible.

Introduction

Thanks for picking up a copy of *30 Ways in 30 Days to a Better Life.*

In my first two books, *162 The Almost Epic Journey of a Yankees Superfan* and *The Last 42,* I tell the story of living out my dreams. In this book, I teach others to live theirs.

I wrote this book in such a way that you can tackle one topic per day. I hope you enjoy the book and the results you'll receive as much as I enjoyed writing it.

I have learned many lessons in my first 47 years of life and business. I hope to share them with you and inspire you to live *your* dreams.

> "Some teachers teach for others to learn. That's not me. Some teachers teach for others to accomplish. That is me."
> – Jim Rohn

We all live an average of 28,000 days. I suggest you use the next 30 days to invest in designing the best life that you can for your remaining days.

– Steve Melia

Contents

We can design our own
life ... or others will
design it for us.

DAY 1

Get Your Day Started Right!

I have made the biggest strides of my life in the shortest amount of time when I was in charge of my day.

How we start our day is simply a habit. First, let's talk about breaking the bad habits.

With modern technology, the phone can control everything we do. This may be the biggest habit I'm going to ask you to break. You can start your day on your terms or someone else's agenda. Put your phone out of reach when you go to sleep. Like, in a different room. Most of us reach for it within seconds of waking up and check our texts, emails, and social media. Some of us are addicted to starting our day with TV, radio, the newspaper, or any communication from the outside world.

I challenge you to break this habit. We receive no value from accessing this information first thing each day. At the very least, we get a short shot of endorphins that quickly fades.

Your thoughts and attitude for the day are immediately formed. The idea is to begin your day from the inside out, not the outside world in. Start now. This is simply a habit. 30 days is all I'm asking. Then, you decide.

Replace this destructive habit by doing the following six things. These will take up to an hour at first, but over time probably closer to 30 minutes.

These six habits will change your life.

Habit #1:

Write down 10-15 goals in a journal or spiral notebook that is designated just for your morning ritual. Begin each day by writing the date at the top. Then answer these questions:

- What do I want?
- What do I want to accomplish?
- What do I want my life to be about?
- Where do I want to go?
- What do I want to create?

Make sure to think big and write down what you desire, not what you think is possible. If you could have, be, do, or accomplish anything, what would that look like?

Here are eight areas that I recommend including:

1. Health and wellness
2. Personal relationships
3. Finance
4. Career
5. Fun/hobbies
6. Travel
7. Spiritual/philanthropic
8. Stuff

Accomplishing goals is the greatest skill I've ever learned, and we will discuss it further in Day 5. Writing your goals down every day turbocharges your efforts and takes them to a new level.

In Grant Cardone's *Be Obsessed or Be Average*, he shares that he has done this every day for years. Leading business expert Brian Tracy says the most successful people he knows start their days, every day, by re-writing their goals. Yes, every day.

I challenge you to begin every day this way for the next 30 days, hopefully longer. Your goals can be short-term or long-term. Do not get caught up in doing this perfectly. Just keep asking yourself, "What do I want my life to be about?"

> "A man is but the product of his thoughts. What he thinks, he becomes."
> – Mahatma Gandhi

Jim Rohn, in his CD series *Take Charge of Your Life*, says, "We can design our lives, or someone will design them for us." Which do you think will be more fulfilling?

This daily regimen will help you write the script for your life.

Habit #2:

Write down at least five things you have accomplished over the last 24 hours that have helped progress one of your goals. I call these Wins!

Examples:

- I exercised for an hour.
- I wrote for 90 minutes.
- I led two powerful conference calls.
- I made 7 sales calls.
- I had a tough conversation.
- I did my personal development.

This will be your daily accountability. Earl Nightingale once said, "Success is a progressive realization toward a worthy ideal." We are happiest when we are accomplishing. Learn to acknowledge your progress.

Habit #3:

Write down at least 5 things you are grateful for. It is hard to get what you want if you are not grateful for what you have. Don't overthink this, keep it simple. We live in an amazing universe.

Habit #4:

Read out loud, with emotion, your affirmations. Here are mine as an example:

- Money flows easily and passively into my life.
- I am divinely guided in all that I do.
- I enjoy inspiring others to live their dreams.
- I am funny and have great timing and delivery.
- I am who I am and I love myself uncon-ditionally, now, and forever.
- I am a best-selling author who loves writing every day.

- I am awake, alive, and I feel great!
- My business is growing every day.

Take a few minutes today and do this. Please make sure to do this step. This is POWERFUL.

What qualities do you want? Simply start each sentence with "I am..." and fill in the blanks.

Reading your affirmations out loud should make you feel better. I had Kelsey Aida Roulades on my podcast, *The 162 Experience,* season 1, episode 29. She wrote the book *#ActuallyICan.*

> "We become what we think about."
> *— Earl Nightinggale*

Feel free to use that episode as a resource to write and shape your affirmations. You can take it a step further and record yourself reading these aloud. Kelsey is a guest author and will go into more detail in Day 8.

Habit #5:

Listen to at least 15 minutes of an inspirational or educational audio or podcast. Sometimes I do this in the background as I complete my other steps. Spaced repetition is how we learn. It can be valuable to listen repeatedly to the same information.

Habit #6:

Read at least 10 pages of a good book. Leaders are readers.

~

At the end of this session, you should feel like you are ready to conquer the world.

Now, and only now, can you go look at your phone or check your email.

DAY 2

Birds of a Feather Flock Together

Whenever I was leaving the house as a teenager, my mom's last words would be, *"Remember who you are."* It was a warning to stay true to my character and not be swayed by the influences of others.

The great Jim Rohn always reminded us, *"Don't join an easy crowd."*

Law of Associations

The laws of associations, much like the laws of gravity, are clear and absolute.

> We become the combined average of our top five associations in all areas of our lives.

It is impossible to be the upbeat, positive, ambitious winner you are destined to be if you are hanging out with five losers.

So, let's take a mental checkup. List your top five associations. They are the inner circle of

> *"People are like elevators. Some bring you up and some bring you down."*
> — *Mike Turpen,* Former Attorney General of Oklahoma and author of Turpen Time

your life, who impact and influence you the most. Simply put a 1-10 on their overall success in life up to this point. Like it or not, you are the average of your five. Yikes!

Let's now ask a few questions. These might sting a little, but the idea is to drastically improve your life over the next 30 days.

- What is the overall health of these five?
- Do they exercise regularly? Do they spend more hours in the gym or in front of their TV?
- How many pounds overweight are they?
- Do they smoke cigarettes? Do they abuse drugs and alcohol?
- Do they make healthy food choices or do they shrug and say it doesn't really matter?
- Do they speak of improving their lives by taking specific action steps?
- Do they read inspirational books?
- Are they encouraging and supportive when you speak of getting better or have a great idea?
- Do they have healthy relationships and get along with their spouses or families?
- Are they happy?
- Do they travel?
- Are they living a life of freedom or are they stuck in the same routine?
- What is their financial picture?
- Do they speak of saving and investing?
- Are they always behind on their bills?
- Do they spend more than they make?

- Do they blame their current circumstances on others or are they more likely to rattle off a good quote, like, "If it is to be, it's up to me?"
- How do they speak of others in their lives, like their co-workers, boss, or friends?
- Are they more likely to complain or tell an uplifting story?
- What is their career track like?
- Are they just getting by or do they speak of doing what they love?
- Do they see the world as abundant and full of opportunity or scarce and not enough to go around?

Some tough questions, huh? How do you think someone would answer these about you?

Like it or not, none of us are strong enough to overcome this law. It is powerful. The first step is to become aware of the effect your associations have on you. The effect can be very subtle. Others are usually just nudging us off course, not yanking us off course.

Next time you are with one of them, notice how they make you feel. Do they want you to become more or shrink down to their size?

When someone is ready to make a change, the things that hold them back the most are the people in their lives and the limiting beliefs and pessimistic attitudes that often go hand in hand.

Here's the good news: you probably know right where to start.

Begin by Improving Your Top 5

Let's look at it like a basketball team. You have your five starters, but are always looking to improve the team.

The five do not have to be people you have direct contact with on a daily basis.

For instance, when I was 24, I discovered Jim Rohn, as well as many other business philosophers and thought leaders. I would begin each day listening to one of his CD programs.

Jim quickly started to impact the way I thought, my attitude, and how I viewed the world. Because of this one improved association, I began to make real changes in my life.

Imagine that! He was now one of my starting five. He was the new point guard leading the charge of my life.

My brother Mike and I were, and still are, business partners. We went on this journey of self-mastery together, so as one of my five, he was growing and getting better, too. Jim Rohn was becoming one of his five as well, as we would listen to him every time we got in the car. If the engine was running, Jim Rohn was playing.

Your job is to continually seek out those who have and want more, and figure out how you can provide value to them in exchange. They are undoubtedly aware of this law, so they may be hesitant to let someone in who may drag down their average.

Your Environment Matters

Our environment matters as well. All environments are different. I was highly blessed to work in an environment of success. Check out some of the studs I had a chance to surround myself with.

At 24, I worked with a start-up company. The CEO was Jeff Olson, author of *The Slight Edge* and one of the biggest builders in the history of direct sales. Over time, we became good friends.

The President was Eric Worre, one of the absolute top trainers in network marketing and founder of GoPro. As I grew in the business, I got his attention, and he also became one of my five.

My sponsor was Darren Hardy. This was before his time as editor and chief of *Success Magazine*, also prior to writing *The Compound Effect*. His wisdom and communication skills still impact me every day.

My brother's best friend and our partner for several years was John Milton Fogg, author of *The Greatest Networker in the World* and renowned expert in network marketing. We would spend hours talking about life and what it took to be successful, while in his hot tub in his mansion in the mountains of Virginia. The point is to put yourself in a winning atmosphere. This includes work, social, and family environments.

The next step is to consider limiting your associations with any of your current five who are bringing down the average. Some people you can spend a few hours with, but not a few days. Some you can spend a few minutes with, but not a few hours.

What is more important to you, their feelings or your future? You don't have to be mean about it. Let them know that you will be spending a lot of time on some exciting new goals you are working on and will not be around as much.

> "If you can't change the people around you, change the people around you."
> — John Addison

This was difficult for me at age 24. Most of my friends and I would hang out and party all weekend. When I started to spend more time working on my business, they gave me a hard time.

Most new projects and businesses take time to get off the ground, and you don't need negative Nancy chirping in your ear. You need someone like-minded, going in a like direction, offering an encouraging word.

Sometimes you have to pull the Band-Aid off altogether and realize certain relationships just aren't serving you.

Walk away. There is probably no easier way to say it. We must make a choice. Them, or being happy. You decide.

DAY 3
The Slight Edge

In changing someone's life, one must change their outlook, or how they think and process information. They must change their philosophies.

I can remember exactly where I was sitting when I saw something called "The Slight Edge" drawn out on an overhead projector in early February of 1995. I was 24 years old and sat in the front row of a ballroom at the Harvey Hotel in Dallas, Texas, with over 1,000 people who were also keen on changing their lives.

I was out of college a couple years and had moved back in with my older sister, Mary, in West Orange, New Jersey. I was her part-time nanny and a struggling entrepreneur. I was hungry. Deep down, I was unsure of myself. I really didn't know if I had what it took to be successful. That is, until I heard about The Slight Edge.

I recommend you read the book, *The Slight Edge*, by the same speaker that day, Jeff Olson, to get the full impact.

The Slight Edge is a philosophy that states:

> "It's the little things that you do that seem to make no difference at all in the act of doing,

but the compound effect over time will lead you to success or failure."

While I was hesitant to believe I could be massively successful, I did buy into the idea that I could do the little things.

Olson and his partner, Worre, explained that the path to success starts with a decision. We make hundreds of decisions a day, all affecting our eventual outcome. Positive decisions, they referred to as simple disciplines. The negative choices were simple errors in judgment. The difference is so small or slight that most people don't think they matter.

Instead, their simple error in judgment was believing success was based on luck, being born into it, or some other factor we have no control over.

I bought into the idea right then that everything matters. Those who exercise the simple disciplines take full responsibility for everything that happens. Everything. Good, bad, or indifferent.

It is empowering to know that all of the choices we have made up to this point have led us to exactly where we are today.

In other words, we got ourselves into this mess, we can get ourselves out. In fact, only we can get ourselves out.

The folks who continually make the simple errors in judgment are more likely to blame when things aren't shaping up the way that they want. They blame the economy, their unsupportive relatives, crooked politicians, inclement weather, and anything else but the real problem—themselves.

Commitment vs. Convenience

Only about 5% of people are consistently making the right choices. This is one reason to go the opposite direction from the herd ... 95% are off track and continue to make simple errors in judgment! What's worse is they will try to convince you to abandon your simple disciplines and join them.

The 5% live their commitments. Commitment is doing the thing you said you would do long after the spirit in which you said it in has left you.

The 95% live a life of convenience. They only make the positive choices when they feel like it, which isn't often enough to make a real difference. In fact, their errors in judgment compound.

Let's take a look at someone who exercises 4 - 5 times per week. They aren't swayed by what month of the year it is or the latest diet fad. They have their regimen and they stick to it, whether they feel like working out that day or not. They are on the slight edge.

Let's look at someone who says they want to be healthier, but let's outside factors interfere. They may say it is too cold to exercise. They may say they are too busy. I heard someone just last week say they didn't join the gym because they didn't like the way it smelled. All excuses are equal. They also are on the slight edge, unfortunately going the wrong direction.

I bought into this idea because it was simple and it made sense. I believed I could get a little better every day. The Japanese call it Kaizan, the ongoing pursuit of continual improvement.

I remember Eric Worre on stage, asking if we thought it was reasonable to get 1/3 of 1% better every day. I nodded along with the crowd. He did the math and the compounded effect would make someone 5000% better in five years.

> "It will take 3-5 years of consistent action to have massive success, or it will take the rest of your life to fail."
> – Jeff Olson

"Count me in," I said to my brother Mike that day, as I embarked on my new life of making positive choices.

"It will take 3-5 years of consistent action to have massive success, or it will take the rest of your life to fail," claimed Olson.

Ouch, that one hurt. My brother and I looked at each other with a knowing eye. We knew, if we kept doing what we had been doing, we would end up exactly where we were at that point...broke.

We decided that very day to change our lives by changing our philosophies. We decided to join the 5% and never look back.

I challenge you to look at all the areas of success we discussed on Day 1 and ask yourself, in what ways are you going the right direction and the wrong direction on the slight edge?

Remember, it starts with becoming aware and continues by consistently exercising simple disciplines. Stay with it long enough and watch your success compound.

DAY 4

Let It Go and Go Grow

Spend a few minutes today reflecting on the people who have been a part of your journey.

On Thanksgiving Day, we don't gather up our clothes, designer watch, new car, and other material goods in the dining room and celebrate.

We do gather our family, friends, and loved ones, though. This is what most of us are the most grateful for.

Be Grateful

I want you to do two assignments today.

Assignment #1

Make a list of all the people who have shaped your journey. This may include your family, school mates, co-workers, mentors, and anyone else who had a positive influence on you or taught you a lesson.

Take it a step further and make a video and post it on social media thanking them and referencing the impact they had on you. This was so uplifting for me, and it's a great way to re-connect.

Or you can write a note, letting them know how much you appreciate them. I clearly remember a letter I received from my good friend, Patrick, several years ago, thanking me for the impact I had on his life 20 years earlier, and I'll always be grateful. So, reach out to the people on your list and show your appreciation.

Grudges Get Worse with Age

The opposite of being grateful is holding a grudge against someone. There is a reason it is called baggage. Baggage is heavy, it can weigh you down, and you have to carry it everywhere you go. We think we need our baggage, but it is slowing us down on the road to success.

Assignment #2

Part two of the assignment is pretty simple. Choose one person you have a grudge against and make the decision to let it go and go grow.

Forgiveness is for you to feel better and move on. It's not for them. Maybe the voice in your head is saying, "Yeah, but they…"

Let it go. Take a deep breath. Is this grudge serving you?

I am not saying what the other person did is ok. What I am saying is it isn't going to have a hold on you anymore.

I'm sure at least one person is coming to mind.

I had a situation like this a few years ago, in which I wasn't letting go. To compound the problem, other people knew about it and kept offering their condolences, reinforcing that I deserved to be upset.

This was not serving me at all. Whenever I spoke of it, I would get angrier, thus strengthening the grudge and making it worse.

Even though I still wasn't happy with what happened, I decided to let it go. I picked up the phone and asked this person to lunch. I apologized for my part in how I handled it and let them know I was over it and that we could move on. I wasn't looking for anything from them.

Is your grudge serving you?

It felt great. In fact, I can think of three people now who I am close with again as a result of this exercise.

I want you to pick up the phone and call your grudge. Chances are, they won't even answer, so you should prepare your message.

Take responsibility for your part. For example:

> "Hey John, it's Steve Melia calling. I know we haven't spoken in a while, and I wanted to apologize for everything that happened. I am embarrassed about how I handled things. When I reflect on all of the people I care the most about, you are at the top of the list. I am

sincerely sorry for what happened between us and I just wanted to take the first step of moving on. If you ever want to chat, I am here to talk. I appreciate you and hope to hear from you."

Or maybe they answer. If this is the case, just say you are sorry for your part in things and do not try to recap what happened or who was to blame. This isn't about right or wrong.

This is for you to feel better. In many situations, the first step is all that is needed to move forward.

Whether you want to be friends again or not isn't important. You will have a huge weight lifted off of you. Let go and be free.

DAY 5

You Are the Author of Your Life

To achieve goals, we must set them.

When you set goals, there will be one of two outcomes. At first, you will probably fail at reaching many of them. Sounds encouraging, right?

But much like anything, you will get better. Your focus and intensity will increase. If you want it bad enough, you will eventually reach your goals.

The big factor is your level of desire. The more you want it, the more patience you will have, and finally, when you show the universe you are serious and not going away, your goals will come to pass.

At age 23, Mike would constantly ask me about my goals. I was so scared just to write down a goal.

Why?

I was afraid to put it out there and not achieve it. What's up with that? I was more concerned with what others thought than my own happiness.

Stop being concerned with what others think and stop comparing yourself to others. My dad used to say,

"People don't think about you as much as you think they do, if at all."

One of the first goals I finally committed to paper was to earn $100,000 per year. It took me five years, but the good news is I blew by that and I never earned less.

Goal-setting uses the imagination to see things that aren't there yet. Imagination is a muscle, and must be used like other muscles. The more you use it, the stronger it will become.

On Day 1, the assignment was to write down 10-15 goals every day. How are you doing on that so far?

If you are new to goal-setting, it is important just to get started and get in the routine of thinking about what you want and writing it down.

Let's take a look at the different types of goals.

Here are some of mine. I want you, right now, to stop and write down at least one goal for each category I have provided.

Health:

- I am in the best physical shape of my life, weighing a solid 180 lbs. with ripped abs, huge, hulk-like, well-defined muscles, and less than 10% body-fat, now and forever.

Career:

- We are earning over $300,000 per month by protecting families with LegalShield and empowering other entrepreneurs to live their dreams and be free, on or before _____.

- I am a *NYT* best-selling author and have written and published 10 books on or before _____.

- My 162 book has sold more than 1,000,000 copies worldwide as of _____.

- The 162 Experience has produced 1,000 episodes, inspiring my listeners to live their dreams. Within five years, it is one of the top ten downloaded podcasts in the world. I have had Tony Robbins, Aaron Judge, CC Sabathia, Reggie Jackson, Dave Chappell, John Mayer, Lewis Howes, Tim Ferris, Jimmy Fallon, Jack Canfield, and Chris Guillibreu on the show.

Financial:

- I have $1,000,000 saved and invested on or before _____.

- I have paid for Macie Grace's college education in full.

Relationship:

- I am in a loving relationship with someone who I adore and loves me for who I am. We have two healthy, bright children. I have an amazing relationship with my daughter, Macie Grace. I am happy in all areas of my life.

Travel:

- I travel to at least two new countries every year.

- I have been to Australia, Ireland, Asia, and Africa on or before _____.

Hobbies/Fun:

- I have thrown out the first pitch at Yankee Stadium and have been featured on The Tonight Show with Jimmy Fallon for breaking my own record of attending 176 consecutive NY Yankee games on or before _____.

Spiritual / Charity:

- We have raised over $100,000 this year for Work Play Love. Our annual Super Bowl fundraiser has raised over $25,000 every year and is growing.

Thank you for letting me share a few of my goals with you! I took out the deadline dates so that no matter when you are reading this book it will be relevant, but clearly it is important that your goals have deadlines.

Take authority for how your life goes. Nobody cares about it as much as you. You are the *"author"* of your life. You can design your life or someone can design it for you. Choose option one and it will be way more fulfilling.

S.M.A.R.T. Goals

Specific / Measurable

Don't be vague. Goals should be as specific as possible. Instead of saying "I want to lose weight," write down exactly how much you will weigh. Rather than saying "I want to earn more," commit to a number. Notice how I wrote we are earning over $300,000 per month. You don't want to limit yourself.

Achievable / Realistic

Many in the success field advise that your goals should be realistic. I think realistic is relative, and certainly do not want to stop the next billion-dollar idea or cure for cancer.

I think a better word is believable. You must believe they are at least possible. If not, you probably won't take any action. If you don't take any action, your belief in yourself will go down as well. So, if you have a huge goal, it may be better to break it down into more believable milestones.

Do you know anyone else who has accomplished your goal or a similar one? For instance, let's say your goal was to complete an ironman. Thousands of athletes do this every year. Maybe your goal is to become a millionaire. There are now more millionaires than at any point in history.

These might be huge goals, but they are possible, as others have already achieved them.

Playing for the NY Yankees at 47 or becoming President of the United States, for me, would probably not be achievable.

It can only be believable if it is achievable, or you won't take the first step.

For instance, my goal is to inspire millions through my books, podcast, message, and lifestyle. A more concrete goal is:

- I have 1,000 super fans who I inspire on a regular basis. They use my coaching as a catalyst to reach their goals.

I can see and believe 1,000 more easily.

Timeline
Goals should have a timeline. I like writing on or before a certain date, in case I accomplish them earlier than expected.

They say 80% of most tasks or projects get done in the last 20% of time. It is important to set milestones or smaller goals along the way.

I have found that 90-day goals are the most useful, because we can see out 90 days and it causes a sense of urgency. Once you have a 90-day goal, you could break it down and set a goal for two weeks. You never want to feel like you have all the time in the world, because it doesn't inspire any action.

The 3 Ps: Present Tense, Post, and Proclaim

I recommend you write the goals as already having been accomplished, in the **present tense**. When writing goals, stay away from "I want" or "I'd like to have." You are telling your subconscious you don't have those things yet.

Make sure to **post** your goals everywhere. We become what we think about most of the time. Print out your goals and tape them in places where you are likely to see them all day, such as your car, bathroom, desk, or kitchen.

Put an alarm on your phone that displays as a written goal. Make your screensaver for your laptop and phone your top goals.

Proclaim your intentions to anyone who will listen. The more people who know about it, the more likely you are to follow through. The more public, the better.

Want to Super Charge Your Goals?

I do have one secret weapon, if there is a goal you absolutely, positively MUST achieve.

A few years ago, my partners and I felt stuck in our business. I guess complacent would be a better word. We were doing fine financially, but our business wasn't growing. It was only maintaining.

About the same time, I saw *NYT* best-selling author Ken Blanchard speak at the ranch of Paul J. Meyer in Waco, Texas. Ken was speaking to a group of about 30 of us on taking our businesses to the next level. He said you are either growing or dying ... you can't be doing both.

If those were the only two choices and I had to be honest, I'd say we were dying. It was time for something drastic.

I also learned from Tony Robbins we are all motivated by the fear of loss or the anticipation of gain. Pain or pleasure. We had gotten to the point where we were very comfortable. The desire of gain wasn't as hot as it once was. This will happen to you when you reach your goals. It is important to keep setting new ones and reach for more.

So here is what we did, and it worked.

We set a very high goal over the next three months, but instead of there being a reward for hitting it, we set a negative consequence if we didn't.

My consequence would have been to jump out of an airplane, thus overcoming my intense fear of heights.

My partner Kim Melia had recently watched the documentary, *"Super-Size Me,"* and would have had to eat a Big Mac for 30 straight days. If you know her, you are aware that her health and wellness is a major priority, and she hasn't visited a McDonald's in the two decades I have known her.

My brother Mike would have had to shave his head completely bald, which isn't his best look, and would have drastically cramped his very busy social life.

We were committed.

Sort of like a ham and egg sandwich. The chicken is involved, but the pig is committed.

We were all in.

The next three months were exhilarating. We hadn't been so inspired in years, and it got us back to the hyper-growth stage.

> ## How committed are you to achieving your goals?

Any time we thought about slowing down or slacking off, I would see an airplane, or Kim would envision a McDonald's, or Mike would see a bad toupee.

I did the same exercise many years later. I needed to get back to the fundamentals and recruit like the old me.

I set a very aggressive goal, and my consequence was to eat an entire can of Alpo dog food if I fell short. I called it The Alpo challenge. I carried a can of Alpo with me everywhere as a constant reminder.

I hit that goal. Are you surprised? Probably not. Because the cost was too much. As you'd imagine, I worked like crazy to reach that goal.

This isn't for everybody, but if you feel stuck and need some extra motivation, give this a try. Make sure you pick something that terrorizes you, then be committed to doing it if you fail. I dare you.

These are some basics of goal-achieving. I hope your dreams are big enough to make this a life-long project. I encourage you to continue to study and practice goal-achieving and make this a part of your life.

DAY 6

Doing Leads to Doing and Waiting Leads to Waiting

The law of momentum states that an object in motion tends to stay in motion. The law of inertia states that an object at rest tends to stay at rest.

Or, as I like to say, doing leads to doing and waiting leads to waiting. This means NOW is always the best time to get started.

For you and I to reach our goals, there is a lot of work to do. Having a great attitude, knowing what we want, and hanging out with the right people are all important elements, but faith without work is dead.

We must develop a get it done attitude.

The less time between thinking of an idea and going to work to implement it, the more likely we are to accomplish it. In other words, when you have a good idea, act on it right away. I call this inspired action.

5.4.3.2.1 ... Blast Off

I've seen Mel Robbins speak live three times over the last year and consumed her book *The 5 Second Rule*. She first shared this idea on TED Talks, and it has become of the most watched episodes ever. Her message is this: when you think of something or you know you have to do something, immediately begin counting down like a rocket ship, and at blast off ... just do it.

The mind can only think of one thing at a time (at least mine can). It is quite normal, when you first think of an idea, to immediately talk yourself out of it. When we begin the countdown, though, we stop talking ourselves out of it.

5.4.3.2.1 ... take action!

I recently thought of someone who I really owed a phone call to. My next thought was Mel Robbins and her simple technique. Within a few seconds, I had dialed the phone and bam! I did it, and it felt great. Mel is one of the most booked speakers in the world today. I want you to try this simple idea today. As soon as you have the thought to do something, 5.4.3.2.1 — Action!

It sounds easy, and it is. It actually is brilliant, and I use it all of the time to overcome procrastination.

Just like the law of momentum, confidence breeds confidence. When you feel good about accomplishing even a small task, keep it going. Make another call, keep writing, or whatever that looks like for you.

As I am writing this book, I get up at a certain time, sit at my kitchen table, and just start writing. The more I write, the more I write.

If I hesitate, it leads to more hesitating. If I make excuses, you get the picture.

Procrastination, the ability to put things off, is the number one killer of all great ideas. The more you do it, well, the more you keep doing it. Mike and I were great at this when we first began working together. Until, one day, we saw the vision of what we could accomplish and what our lives could be like if we went to work.

"If the picture is clear, the price is easy," we heard our mentor, Jim Rohn, proclaim. It starts one action at a time. Then another. Then another. Until, one day, you begin to develop the reputation of someone who gets things done. We began to be known as "the brothers."

They weren't calling us "the brothers" for being lazy and not taking care of business. They were calling us "the brothers" because we were making things happen.

The only thing better than taking action is SSMA:

Short-term Speedy Massive Action.

Get started and work like crazy. Every time you take a break or stop, it is much harder to get going again.

In physics, when your read about momentum, it speaks of how energy is created. The more action, the more energy. There is no energy created with inertia.

Start today by acting on your ideas right away. Make decisions. Make the tough calls. Make things happen. Create the life you want by taking massive action repeatedly and watch your life change for the better.

DAY 7

Use the Law of Attraction to Get What You Want

What are you thinking about?

Brian Tracy says, "You will attract the people, ideas, and resources that are in harmony with your most dominating thoughts."

If you are judging how things are, then you are thinking about the past, because those things have already been created based on what you attracted in the past. If we want things to change, we need to change what we are thinking about and how we are thinking about them.

Let's start with the people we are attracting. Look at your top associations, as we discussed in Day 2. In what ways do you think you may have attracted these folks?

Some are probably obvious because of having the same interests, or maybe they live close to you.

Let's talk about attracting the right people we want in our lives. Whether it be business, personal relationships, or meeting new friends, it works the same.

What are the top five qualities you would like them to have? Do you want them to be ambitious? Positive? Goal-oriented? The best way to attract these qualities is to work on ourselves. Be the person you want to attract.

Life gets better on the outside when we get better on the inside. We tend to attract the people in our lives who we deserve based on our personal and professional development.

> Life gets better on the outside when we get better on the inside.

We attract the results as well. Focus on what you want! What most people do is worry or focus on what they don't want. This attracts more of the same. Successful people focus on what they want.

Visualize

Visualizing is creating a clear picture in your mind of your goal, materialized. This is as easy as sitting down with your eyes closed and imagining your goal completed.

Here are a few things to help.

Frequency

This is how often we think about what we want already accomplished.

Duration

This is how long we visualize for.

Intensity

The more emotionally charged it is, the more real it will seem. Your subconscious mind doesn't know the difference between our imagination and reality.

Utilize as many of the senses as possible when picturing your ultimate goal completed.

- How do you feel?
- What sounds are nearby?
- Can you hear the crowd cheering for you as you are giving your big speech?
- What do you see?
- What people do you notice there?
- What would shaking their hand be like?
- What smells do you notice?

Our minds are powerful. Put the odds in your favor by being laser focused on creating the life you want.

In the next chapter on affirmations, I've asked my friend, author and blogger Kelsey Aida Roualdes, to share how the law of attraction and affirmations work together.

DAY 8

Actually I Can
By Kelsey Aida Roualdes

If you think you're new to affirmations, think again.

Everyone is constantly affirming things, whether it is out loud or in their head. Things like, "I suck at math," "I'm just a lucky person," and "I can't afford it" are all affirmations.

Basically, affirmations are synonymous with self-talk. To affirm just means "to state or assert positively," or to "maintain as true." Therefore, an affirmation can be anything you say (or think) to yourself, or anyone else for that matter!

Now, whether or not yours are improving or diminishing your life is a whole other story.

When we talk about using affirmations as a tool for a better life, we are talking about deliberately making positive, helpful affirmations. When used properly, these kinds of affirmations can make a HUGE impact on your life.

Take my story for example. I used to have dysthymia depression for three years. And when I did, I was always affirming how depressed I was, how much I hated my life, and so on … but as soon as I shifted my mindset and realized I was not my depression, everything changed. The simple affirmation, "I am not my depression," was the kick starter for me to start healing.

Fast forward a few years from then, and now I'm an inspirational blogger who is teaching people how to own their power and win at life, I'm one of the happiest people I know, AND I've even written a whole book on affirmations called *#ActuallyICan: The Art of Affirming Yourself to Greatness*!

So, I think it's safe to say affirmations can help produce some pretty powerful results!

The "Fake It till You Make It" Approach

Most affirmation books, teachers, and resources of the like will all tell you the same thing:

Fake it till you make it.

Essentially, they want you to repeat affirmations that sound good on the outside, but feel bad on the inside until, somehow (magically), they change your life.

This approach looks something like this. You are poor, but you want to be rich, so you stand up in front of your bathroom mirror, look yourself in the eyes, and "confidently" state to the Universe, "I am a wealth magnet!" You continue to do this exercise every day for a month, yet, for some reason, your bank account still says otherwise … frustrating, right?

Well, think about this: if you were in this situation, how would you really feel when you stated the affirmation? Would you actually feel rich just because your words say so? Or would you just feel like a big fat liar?

Probably the latter. And that's why this approach is a complete waste of time.

The problem with this approach is that it never works because the real power of an affirmation is not necessarily the words in it, but how it makes you feel when you say it. So, if it just makes you feel stupid, or like a liar, then you're not helping your life much, are you?

The key to successfully using affirmations is to be able to feel good (or at least a little better) when you think or say them. Because, when you change your mood, you change your vibes, and when you change your vibes, you change your life.

What you want to do is find or create affirmations that are about your goals, and still feel good to say. You want to be able to really get behind the affirmation, with confidence and authenticity.

Sticking with the same example, here's what that would look like in practical terms. Instead of trying to affirm you are a "wealth magnet," you could affirm something like:

- "Every day I am expanding my knowledge when it comes to making money."
- "I am open to having more money in my life."

- "I'm ready to start bringing in more money than ever before."

Feel the difference?

These affirmations are still supporting your ultimate goal of becoming rich, but when you say them, you can actually believe in yourself and feel empowered instead of stupid. :)

Why Affirmations Work

Most people think the affirmation in and of itself is what creates change in one's life. "If I just affirm that I'm in a loving relationship enough times, it will eventually come true ... right?"

While there is massive creative power in your words, the real power of affirmations lies in their ability to change or enhance your *mood*.

Your mood is what determines your point of attraction when it comes to the Law of Attraction. Since the Law of Attraction states like energy attracts like energy, and your mood is a direct indicator of your energy in any given moment, the higher or better your mood, the higher or better your point of attraction.

In simpler terms, when you feel good, you'll be a match to attracting more feel-good things, and when you feel bad, (you guessed it) you'll be an energetic match to attracting more things that make you feel bad.

Like you learned yesterday, you attract what you focus on. So, when you focus on positive affirmations, (A.K.A. how you want things to be) you WILL get them. The true power of affirmations is in the feeling they give you, the focus they require, and lastly, the power of their words.

How to Use Affirmations (Successfully)

There are many fun and easy ways to use affirmations in your daily life, which is part of the reason why I think they are such a great tool. Here are a few of my personal favorites to help get you started today!

Step #1 – Write them down.

There is something extremely powerful about writing down, BY HAND (this is key), the way you intend your life to be. Go through all the main areas of your life one-by-one and list out a few positive affirmations about each one. Your paper may look something like this…

Finances:
- I am working toward a better financial future for me and my family.
- I love the idea of passive income.
- I'm ready to adopt an abundance mentality from now on.

Health:
- I treat my body with love and care.
- I am grateful for my health.
- My body knows how to heal itself.

Relationships:

- I am thankful for all the wonderful people in my life.
- I love making new friends and contacts who want to help and see me succeed.

Life (in general):

- I love my life!
- I'm content with what is and excited for what's to come.
- Life flows easily for me.

Basically, you are turning your goals into affirmations and writing them down as if they are already happening. You do this by using only the present tense.

Step #2 – Mediate with them.

This is a super simple meditation you can use on a daily basis to check off meditation and affirmations from your self-help to do list all at once! All you do is this. As you breathe in, you think an affirmation that feels nice, and as you breathe out, you think another affirmation that also feels nice. Easy!

It looks something like this...

- Inhale: I am thankful.
- Exhale: My life is awesome.
- Inhale: I love feeling good.
- Exhale: Feeling good is my natural state of well-being.
- Inhale: I feel peaceful.

- Exhale: I feel calm.

Or, if you don't want to make up new affirmations the whole time, you can just stick with two and keep them on repeat. You use one for all your inhales and another for all your exhales. One of my personal favorite affirmation combos is this one.

- Inhale: I am love.
- Exhale: I am light.

Step #3 – Spam your life with them.

If there is an affirmation, or a few in particular you really resonate with at the moment, write it/them down on a sticky note and put it/them somewhere you will see them often throughout your day. This could be on your bathroom mirror, your fridge, your computer, your car dashboard ... wherever! Feel free to get creative with this one.

Personally, I like to pick an affirmation of the week and write it directly on the big mirror in my room. That way, every morning when I wake up, I can mentally or verbally recite the affirmation as I look at myself in the mirror (a powerful affirmation practice to try).

A Few Rules to Keep in Mind

In order for your affirmations to work, I want you to keep these few very important rules in mind as you start your affirmation journey. Whenever trying to pick an affirmation, use this checklist as a tool to make sure it passes the test as a successful affirmation.

1. The affirmation has to feel good when you think/say it.
2. The affirmation has to be in the present tense, as if it is already happening.
3. The affirmation has to be about what you do want, not what you don't want. (Meaning, it is written in the positive, not the negative.)

Whether or not you're new to affirmations, I challenge you to find or create three (or more) you love and start using them on a daily basis. Then, pick one of the ways mentioned above to start incorporating them into your daily life!

If you need help discovering or brainstorming affirmations, visit my blog at kelseyaida.com or get my book *#ActuallyICan: The Art of Affirming Yourself to Greatness*.

DAY 9

Live Out of Your Comfort Zone

Everything we want is on the other side of our comfort zone. Does simply thinking about a goal make you uneasy? If it doesn't, maybe it isn't big enough.

With The Slight Edge principle, we learned that we must embrace discomfort to one day become comfortable.

As a former smoker, I can attest to the severe pain of withdrawals one must go through so one day we can do simple activities, like walk up a flight of stairs without looking like we just ran a marathon.

We must always give up a small piece of what we want to get our ultimate goal. We invest money to make more. We work hard and give up our time to earn time freedom.

Jim Rohn explains that there are two ways to approach the future. One is with anticipation and the other is with apprehension. We can welcome the discomfort or shy away from it and keep things the way they are.

Change, or doing things we've never done before, is always awkward. Public speaking, talking to the opposite sex, making our first sales call, and driving a stick shift are all examples of doing things out of your comfort zone.

Expand the Zone

The longer you can stay out of this zone, the more you are going to grow. My brother Mike and I were living with our sister Mary, sharing one bedroom in her house in November of 1994.

We stayed out of our comfort zone for much of the time over the next three years. We set huge goals and we did things every day that made us feel uneasy. Because of the small sacrifice of comfort, we live a very different life today.

"Always do what you are afraid to do."
– Ralph Waldo Emerson

Success breeds success. The ripple effect of operating out of your comfort zone is that you are more likely to do it again and for longer periods of time until it becomes more natural.

In my first days as a public speaker, I would experience severe anxiety days before taking the stage. I was severely out of my comfort zone. Today, I speak to crowds regularly of hundreds and thousands.

Just like anything, you get a little bit more comfortable each time. What is happening? Your comfort zone is expanding. You get a little better. You gain confidence. You soon gain competence, and voila!

One day, the thing that caused so much angst becomes easy. Speaking in front of large audiences today is one of my favorite things to do. I would have never been able to experience this joy if I wasn't able to live out of my comfort zone. We don't serve the world by playing small.

Consider these words in "Our Deepest Fear" from Marianne Williamson:

> "Our deepest fear is not that we are inadequate. Our deepest fear is that we are powerful beyond measure. It is our light, not our darkness that most frightens us. We ask ourselves, Who am I to be brilliant, gorgeous, talented, fabulous? Actually, who are you not to be? You are a child of God. Your playing small does not serve the world. There is nothing enlightened about shrinking so that other people won't feel insecure around you. We are all meant to shine, as children do. We were born to make manifest the glory of God that is within us. It's not just in some of us; it's in everyone. And as we let our own light shine, we unconsciously give other people permission to do the same. As we are liberated from our own fear, our presence automatically liberates others."

I can vividly remember the pain of approaching the opposite sex beginning in my mid-teens and continuing through my early twenties.

My voice cracked, my body shook, I stuttered, and I'm sure that I was sweating profusely as well, but I did it. Looking back, I was such a mess that I'm not surprised most of the girls rebuked my efforts. But every single one of those times, I achieved victory. The real victory is embracing the moment and doing it. The short-term results are almost irrelevant.

One of those times was when I was having lunch with one of my most successful friends, Bob Levy. Bob is the founder of Merry-Go-Round boutiques. We were in a deli in Atlanta and there was a very attractive girl in the booth next to us, facing me. We made eye contact repeatedly and smiled back and forth a few times as well.

On the ride back to Bob's, I immediately regretted the decision of not saying anything to her. This was before I owned a cell phone. Upon returning to Bob's, I picked up the phone and awkwardly explained to the deli clerk that I wanted to speak to the red head seated in the second booth on the left.

"What's her name?"

"I don't know it and I'm not sure if she's even still there."

A brief moment later, a voice came on the phone.

"Hello?"

I hadn't even planned what to say. "Hi. So, um, I was sitting across from you ..."

"Is this the guy with the blue eyes?"

Bingo!

The big victory in situations like this is the feeling you get. I was super uncomfortable, but I did it anyway.

In my field of sales and marketing, we must talk to people every day about our products and services.

Some people are more comfortable to prospect than others.

The ones who are way out of our comfort zone, I call your chicken list. These folks are probably really successful, or at least that's our perception. Make those calls. You will grow every time you do it. The only way to it, is through it.

When we set goals for things we've never achieved or things we don't have, tension is created. When you keep operating outside your comfort zone, growth is happening.

> "Do the thing and you'll have the power."
> — Ralph Waldo Emerson

We can quit. That will make the fear or discomfort go away. So will procrastinating. So will doing the thing you fear.

Stay out of the zone.

DAY 10
Work While It's Day

As you sow, so shall you reap.

The mantra of the farmer:

> "Work while it's day, before the sun goes down."

This was the mantra Mike and I subscribed to, which we learned from Jim Rohn early in our career.

You can make up in numbers what you lack in skill. You can win by outworking the competition. Do more than you get paid for, and one day you will get paid for more than you do.

One thing you have 100% control over is your work ethic. Whether you are the CEO of your own company or not, treat it that way, and chances are you will be the CEO one day. Choose to be the CEO of your own life.

Develop the reputation of having a great work ethic. Let's revisit the sowing example. What you can control is how many seeds you plant and what your attitude is like in the process.

In the formula for all success, there is sowing and reaping. We must first plant, then cultivate, and finally, harvest. The more we plant, the greater our harvest will be.

Our work ethic will determine how much, how often, and how effective we become at planting and cultivating. So, as Jim Rohn tells us, "The guy says 'I really need to reap,' then you really need to plant."

Your long-term vision and reasons must be powerful. The promise for tomorrow must be clear, if we are to enroll in the activities of today.

When you see someone "mailing it in," which means they are slacking off or just showing up and doing the minimum without any passion, it is usually a sign that they do not love what they do. Unfortunately, this represents much of North America today.

When you love what you do and are connected to the result, you work harder to make things happen. You care about winning.

Don't Go Bowling in the Spring

This was a mantra of ours in the early days. Imagine if you asked this of a farmer. He'd laugh. It's time to plant.

For you, bowling might be the TV, social media, fantasy football, or binge watching on Netflix. Do a quick inventory of your life and how you spend your time. There are 168 hours in a week. We all have the same amount time. It is all about priorities.

Whose dream are you building? Are you building your favorite musician's dream or your own? Some people get more excited about cheering for their local sports team than they do about their own life.

Just Say NO

One of the reasons to share your goals with those closest around you is so you can set boundaries. I have worked from home since age 23. People will assume you are not busy, or that they can ask you to do all sorts of favors. Learn to say no. Protect your time.

How much do you think you are really worth per hour when you are doing your highest payoff activity? Treat it that way.

DAY 11

Giving Is Living
By Kim Melia

We have all heard your why has to make you cry. I have several *"whys."* For the purpose of this chapter, I'd like to share some of my story and why I believe giving is living.

I was born in Edmonton, Canada in 1972. My only real memory of my biological father was that he was a very abusive and violent man. He would constantly beat my mother and two older brothers. Though I was young and didn't receive as much of the abuse, I still remember the fear I had of him. It still haunts me.

Thank God my amazing mother had the courage to pack our bags and move us out. I don't know where I would be today if it wasn't for that brave act. I was only three years old when we left, but I remember telling myself the bad man was gone. Gone, but not forgotten.

It was only a few months later when my mother would meet the man I call Dad today. Tom Lloyd is one of the greatest people who ever came into my life. He was every child's dream dad. I suppose he restored my faith that not all men were monsters.

It was always comforting knowing I could go to him for anything, and his unconditional love poured into our family.

So, when he and my mom brought all of us kids to our favorite restaurant and sat us down to tell us they were separating, it was one of the most devastating days of my life. I immediately became angry and decided I would do what I wanted to do from that point on. I spiraled out of control.

I was 13 years old, living life with no purpose. I was a rebel without a cause. I was a punk rocker, hanging around all the wrong people, skipping school, doing drugs, and I only cared about where the next party was going to be.

My wakeup call was finding my good friend dead in a dumpster from a drug overdose. This was my turning point. I knew if I didn't change, I'd be next.

I immediately got focused on becoming a better me. I started listening to my parents. I focused on school and got my grades up. I totally changed my network of friends, and I was the first to graduate from high school in my entire family.

Although I turned my life around, tragedy still struck my family. At 21, I found my mom's live-in boyfriend, who had committed suicide, in our garage. I'm still frightened by loud noises and sirens.

My boss told me I needed to be at work the next day because he was not in my immediate family. Another defining moment. I knew right then and there, corporate Canada and having a normal job wasn't the path for me. No one was going to tell me how long I could grieve for.

I started to look for ways I could work from home. Two true angels came into my life, Rob and Charlene Mackenzie. They became my first real mentors and taught me how to be my own boss. This led me to meet the Melia Brothers.

> "To those whom much is given, much is expected."
> – Anonymous

Even before this episode, I recall feeling a little empty in my life. I guess I was searching when I happened to see a sign asking for people to volunteer for a group called Child Find. We would take the fingerprints and footprints of babies in case they were ever abducted or lost. About a year later, I found another opportunity to volunteer for a suicide awareness hotline.

This was before any of the many suicide attempts that happened in my family. It was a way for me to give back to the troubled. I had a very close connection and understanding of what they were going through.

When my mother's boyfriend committed suicide, I had to stop working as a volunteer at the suicide awareness hotline. It was too much to handle. This made me do some serious soul-searching.

Fast forward to my mid-twenties. We were blessed that our business was becoming fairly successful. I began to accumulate all of the trappings of success. I was checking goals off my list, such as nice cars, a big house, exotic vacations, and time freedom.

Something was missing, though. You learn quickly that happiness doesn't come from "things."

A good friend, David Stecki, was dying of cancer. We were inspired by Dave's attitude of gratitude during his final weeks and days. A group of us were able to raise a significant amount of money to help with his bills in a relativity short time.

My calling had met my skill set. I realized I was very good at raising money. I enjoyed the thrill of having an idea and seeing it through. I am in a very visible business with a large social network and have been able to use my platform to do good.

Over the next several years, we began to donate a large amount of our time and resources to various charities.

We worked with the Boys and Girls Club implementing a success for teens program, raised $25,000 for suicide awareness, and were named the volunteers of the year.

We also raised tens of thousands of dollars for the Make-A-Wish foundation and volunteered in many different capacities.

I was being fulfilled in a way I had never experienced before. For me, if I wasn't giving, I wasn't living. My life went from being empty to being full. Full of gratitude. Full of amazing experiences and heartfelt relationships. I began to attract other givers, and soon this became a huge part of our business's culture.

Where Do I Start?

There are many ways to give back. It doesn't have to be donating money. Just start somewhere. Pick something close to your heart. Volunteering is a great place to see what feels right for you.

There are lots of great places to volunteer your time. Local churches, food banks, shelters, elderly centers, animal shelters, Earth Day, running in a charity race, helping with a fundraiser, becoming a big sister or big brother, and taking care of people in your family who need support are just a few of thousands of options. Just pick one.

The best way to appreciate your own life is to help others with their lives. This helped me see how much I have to be grateful for. It feels amazing to give back to your community and universe.

I am now co-founder of a nonprofit called workplaylove.org. My business partner Mike Melia ran into a flight attendant who supported an orphanage in Guatemala. Soon after that happenstance meeting, we found ourselves on a plane to Guatemala to check out these sweet kids and see where our money would be going.

Our Hearts Have No Borders

It has been almost a decade now that I have been going to Guatemala, and each year I spend about three months supporting and loving these amazing children. We work on various projects, we play all day long, and we love them unconditionally.

Initially, we met a huge goal and helped raise $72,000 in 90 days to build a girls orphanage, adjacent to an existing boys orphanage. We now work directly with the administrators, helping them set up their annual budget. Through our Hogar Heroes program, we are able to pay for all the costs to run the girls orphanage, which houses 25 little princesses, while also supporting the attached boys orphanage and the village kids. The Hogar Heroes is a monthly tithing program we set up to help meet their financial needs.

It is such a blessing to be part of these kids' lives. One of the best parts is our relationships with the children and caretakers. I have a very strong bond with many of them, as I have made it a priority to consistently spend quality time with these children.

Our involvement helps these kids have hope and believe that they are important in a world that seems so unfair, and lets them know they have a chance in life. I know what it is like to feel abandoned.

The Ripple Effect

One of the first boys I met was 9-year-old Erick. Erick loves playing music in his church band, and we hit it off right away. We developed a very close bond within the first two years, but unfortunately, he was moved to another orphanage. It was so hard to see him go. We were disconnected for about a year, but I made sure I wrote him and also made special trips to visit.

I committed to myself to stay in his life. He lets me know when he hits a milestone at school, church, or with his music. We continue to have conversations and we see each other as much as possible.

I never really knew the impact of our bond until I received a sweet note from Erick, recently. Tears rolled down my cheeks as he told me how I touched his life and helped him believe in himself and his abilities. His English is a little broken.

> "Thanks Kim. I was given the privilege of playing in the church again. I hope that in my life I am given the opportunity to jump to fame and thus be able to help homes and people like you do. Thanks for believing in me. I hope the world needs me with my talent, I love you, I hope to see you soon. You are like my family to me. I want to repeat the love and blessings that you've shown me, you are a great example to follow. I love you."

At 17, he wants to dedicate his life to giving back to the underprivileged orphans in Guatemala.

This is what the ripple effect means to me. You never know who's watching and who will be inspired to pay it forward. I feel like I have been blessed because of these children. They have helped me become so much more than I could've ever imagined and have given me the strength to continue to serve and to grow into the best person I could be. They fill my cup up when it's empty. I could never have imagined being so fulfilled, feeling I have a purpose here on this earth, and I live with so much gratitude in my life every day.

We love to bring volunteers to Guatemala. It is a game changer. A life changer. One of my friends' 13-year-old daughters, Kylie, was being bullied at school. She was also dealing with the fact that one of her schoolmates had taken her own life. Like many teens, Kylie was going through a rough time.

I reached out to her parents and invited Kylie to come on our next trip. She came with her mom, and since then has become a beacon of light to herself and her friends. She's actively involved in her church, her grades are up, she continues to fundraise for many different charities, and she is even doing motivational speeches at 14. She began appreciating her own life more, and in turn, wanted to serve and help as many in need as possible.

We have also inspired others to open up their own nonprofits as they've watched us through the years. Now, they feel so much purpose in their lives, to be able to give back in their own way and have an even greater impact on the world.

If I could turn my life around and make a positive difference, so can you. If you ain't giving, you ain't living.

DAY 12
Get a Coach

To win in sports, business, and life, we must take full advantage of every resource possible.

All great winners have a coach.

Here is one formula for massive success my friend Brian Carruthers wrote about in his book, *Building an Empire.*

Burning desire
+
Great work ethic
+
Coachable spirit
=
Massive Results

I saw a sign in a gym that read: *Check your ego at the door.* Sometimes, when someone's ego is too big, they don't think they can learn from anyone else. Ugh, a know-it-all. With this philosophy, one will only go so far.

Behind every champion is a team. Behind every great team is a great coach.

We all need someone who can stand behind us and watch and help us course correct. They see our blind spots. They challenge us, encourage us, and hold us accountable, even when we don't feel like going on.

It's easier to quit on ourselves than to quit on our team or coach.

They often believe in us more than we believe in ourselves. How many times do we hear a mega-successful athlete refer to a childhood moment when a coach made all of the difference?

Think of one your most important goals right now. Ask yourself, has anyone ever done what you want to do? What is their track record? Have they won before? What are their motivations? Is this someone you like being around? Will you get better or more results by hiring this person?

Have you ever had a personal trainer? I have had several over different periods of my life. I can tell you, when I'm in charge of the workout, it is way different than when I have a trainer.

One of my trainers in San Diego would have this line he would use when he could tell I was apprehensive when he was adding more weight on the bars or machine.

> "Steve, I am like a mathematical genius when it comes to this stuff. Based on what you've already lifted and the amount of reps you've

done, I know exactly what you are now able to do."

Made sense to me, so with that little boost of confidence, I would momentarily focus and accomplish that next goal. I believed that he believed I could win. Sometimes, that is all you need.

You could also call this person a mentor. Mentors take all forms, and sometimes can serve as a coach. Sometimes we call someone a mentor, but it is from afar. These relationships are helpful as well.

But a coach is hands-on. They are right there on the sidelines. They are watching and growing with you. They are part of your team. They have the same goal as you, for you to win. They know all about you and believe in you.

They may push, yell, and scream because they want it as bad as you.

So, whether it's taking your business to levels you've never seen before, finding the mate who's perfect for you, or winning your course championship, build a winning team by getting a winning coach.

DAY 13

Commitment

In March of 2011, I announced to the world I would be attending all 162 games of the New York Yankees that season. Yep, home and away.

Over the next seven months, everything I did was to honor that fanatical commitment.

As fun as attending all the Yankees games was, it didn't come without me questioning my decision many times. Even the first night of the season.

Here's an excerpt from *162 The Almost Epic Journey of a Yankees Superfan:*

> *Friday April 1st – Am I a Fool?*
>
> *"It's 4 a.m. and I am wide awake. Thoughts of doubt swirl through my head as rain pounds my brother's roof. I had imagined that there would be internal struggle as we moved through the season. I just didn't expect it this early. If I am ever ready to abandon something, the right time would be now. I am seriously considering calling the entire thing off. I guess there are always downs after an up. The euphoria of attending an Opening Day has worn off and I am seriously weighing our next move."*

Our moods and feelings can fluctuate. Commitment doesn't. Amateurs do things when they feel like it; professionals do them because they said they would.

Whether it stems from fear or listening to the unsolicited advice of others, you won't always feel like honoring your commitments.

The opposite of commitment is convenience. Doing what is easy or comfortable.

The funny thing is, you don't hear successful people quoting the definition of convenience very often.

If we only did things when we felt like it, we wouldn't get much done. Think about your job or business. Let's say you work 300 days per year. How many of those 300 did you feel like getting out of bed? Try going in only when you feel like it and you'll probably be looking for work.

> "Commitment is doing the thing you said you would do long after the mood you said it in has left you."
> – Darren Hardy

Sometimes it is easier to be committed if there is an immediate consequence. Like getting fired. When you work for yourself or are focused on seeing your goal through, the buck stops with you.

Writing a book takes commitment. I change my entire schedule when I'm writing. I commit to getting up at

7am and going right to the laptop. When my alarm goes off, I think of my finished product, not how I feel.

When I was 24 and new in my network marketing business, I asked my mentor, "What do I need to do to be successful?"

He said, "Give me 52 Tuesday nights."

We had our business overviews on Tuesdays, and he was letting me know that was one of the most important commitments I would need to make.

All commitment starts with a decision.

You ever ask someone to do something and they respond by saying, "I'll try," or "I'll see what I can do?" It doesn't generate a lot of confidence, does it?

If you've had a challenge keeping your word in the past, make a decision to change that, beginning right now. Decide that no matter what, when you agree to do something, you will see it through. No canceling appointments. No calling in sick. No procrastinating because the game is on. Keep your word.

My friend, Rich Kennedy, in my 162 book, said this about me: "Steve is the kind of person who does what he says he will do. If Steve says he'll do it, consider it done." Those words mean a lot to me!

I can't tell you how empowering it is to have that kind of reputation.

Commit to Less

Only commit to things you intend on doing. Sometimes we can be too nice and over-promise. Or maybe we just don't want to say no. Learn to say no if it doesn't serve you or your bigger vision.

Try this. Someone asks you for a favor you don't want to do. "No, I can't do that, but if that changes, I will let you know." Practice saying no. Eventually, people will stop asking you to do tasks that aren't helping you achieve your goals.

It is easier to commit to things if you only have a few commitments.

What also helps is proclaiming your commitments to as many people as possible. Within one week of deciding to do 162, we were featured on our local news. You can Google WWAY Two Local Comics, if you'd like to watch. Once we were on television, we had come too far.

I am in a business with fairly high turnover. One reason is because it only costs a few hundred dollars to get started. The commitment factor isn't very high. I tell my new recruits to imagine you have invested $500,000 and treat your business that way. If someone laid out that kind of dough, commitment wouldn't be an issue.

It's simple, folks. Do what you say you'll do all the time.

DAY 14

Put the FUN Back in Fundamentals

Well, if you'd made it this far in the book and you've ever studied different personality types, you've probably concluded that I like to have fun. When Mike and I started working together, he gave me the title "Director of Fun." If it's not fun, I just don't want to do it.

Fun is defined as:

> A source of enjoyment, amusement, diversion, etc.

You can tell a lot about how different people will describe the same situation. Whether it's a life-changing weekend, a World Series game, or even the funeral of a beloved friend, I'll often sum it up with "that was fun."

In most projects or goals, you must illicit the efforts of others. People do not like to work in stress-filled environments. People have enough tension at their jobs and at home. They are not looking for any more. Make things fun.

Fun doesn't happen by accident. It is weaved like a fine tapestry.

Every summer, we host an event for our sales force. By design, we make it fun. Periodically, we host theme-related parties. One of the most fun was our Grease-themed dinner/dance. The guys dressed up as T-Birds and the gals as Pink Ladies. As I type this, a huge smile comes across my face as I remember everyone in costume, staying in character.

We have also held Jimmy Buffet parties, hired comedic hypnotists, played the Not-So-Newlywed game, held Country-Western dances, and had our infamous talent show, The Melia Idol.

We have become known as the fun family, or the fun team. We accept that reputation wholeheartedly.

The culture of our families, our businesses, and our companies all have a certain feel to them. Make sure to include fun. This doesn't mean we don't work hard, have big goals, or take our lives seriously. Everything just seems to gel better when it's fun.

Customers would rather shop at a fun store with happy employees. Students would rather learn from a fun teacher who has an entertaining classroom environment. Employees are more likely to stay at a job where they feel appreciated and enjoy coming to work every day.

The bar Cheers from the 1980s sitcom had a fun feel to it.

> Sometimes you want to go where everybody knows your name,

And they're always glad you came;
You want to be where you can see, our troubles are all the same;
You want to be where everybody knows your name.

Teams who play together, stay together. You can spot professional sports teams enjoying themselves. The players are smiling, interacting, high-fiving, and cheering each other on. They want to be there.

Decide to make your life, your business, your goals, and your personal life more fun. Outside of personal experience, I don't have any scientific proof to back this up, but I'm convinced people who are having more fun in their lives will live longer, be healthier, and well, of course, be happier.

Enjoy the ride.

DAY 15

Save the Drama for Your Mama

Our attitudes are not something we can fix just one time. They are fluid. They can change from one moment to the next, and from one day to the next.

Attitudes need to be cultivated. No matter how positive someone seems, we all need to work on it every day. I sure do.

Diseases are contagious. They can start with a small infection and grow into something more severe, or even kill you (or your attitude).

7 Diseases of Attitude

#1 – Indifference

We have all met or know people who just don't seem to care. You can identify this symptom because they shrug their shoulders a lot, like they couldn't care less. I attend a lot of weekend seminars to work on myself and my business. I'll often ask another attendee, "What do you like best so far?" Someone with indifference may just look at me with no passion and shrug. If you want more out of life, you have to care. You have to want it. Live with passion. Don't be afraid to show some emotion.

#2 – Indecision

Successful people are able to make decisions quickly. Unsuccessful people are much slower. They fear making the wrong choice, thus they kill the moment. Remember, doing leads to doing and waiting leads to waiting. If you have a challenge with this one, decide to start deciding things faster. Even if you are wrong, you will know quickly and readjust. You will still be further along than if you just sat stagnant.

Here's an exercise for you. Next time you go to a restaurant, open the menu and find one thing to order. As soon as you see something you'll like, close the menu, set it down, and don't second guess yourself. This little exercise will get you in the habit of making split second decisions.

People will often say, "Let me think about it." Think about what? You have all of the information. You are wasting time. Make a decision and move on.

#3 – Doubt

To feel uncertain about or be afraid of is to doubt ... and nobody wants to be around a doubting person.

The opposite of doubt is confidence. If you want to be a leader, who do you think people want to follow more, a doubter or someone with confidence who believes in themselves and a favorable outcome?

When we doubt, we often won't even take the first step. It's hard to put our spirit behind something if we don't expect it to work. Unfortunately, like the other diseases, doubting can become a habit.

Doubters tend to doubt. Break this habit by looking at a situation and asking, *"If this was going to work, how would it work?"*

What would need to happen to make this outcome favorable? If you want to win in anything, you must believe and expect to win. Opportunity can only knock a few times in your life, and if you have the habit of doubting everything that comes along, you'll probably miss your knock. Be open.

#4 – Worry

I saw a sign in front of a church many years ago and I took a picture and kept it with me. It read:

> Worry is negative goal-setting.

I love that description. When you worry, you think and focus on the worst possible result or outcome while attaching negative emotions.

This is the same formula for getting what we want, but only the opposite. Visualize your goal materialized while attaching positive emotions.

> "Take the first step in faith. You don't have to see the whole staircase, just take the first step."
> – Martin Luther King, Jr.

Whenever you find yourself worrying, take a deep breath and realize this is just a habit and can be broken.

Now, focus on the positive outcome you are hoping for.

The more often and longer you picture in your mind what you want, the sooner you can break this negative thought pattern.

#5 – Overcautious

Someone with this disease is always afraid to take the next step. Maybe they were yelled at a lot as a child, or even as an adult. These folks are gun shy and do want to experience the constant failure we all must experience on the path to success.

We have all heard the principle that the road to success is filled with failure. How can you get anywhere in life if you are always so concerned about taking the wrong step?

Jump and the net will appear.

#6 – Pessimism

Pessimism is the tendency to see the worst aspect of things or believe that the worst will happen. There is simply no hope of a better future!

If you consider yourself a pessimist, I would suggest making a decision to change. Why? Because your future doesn't look very bright, and I predict you will fail miserably.

How did that feel? Yeah, well, we don't like it either.

#7 – Complaining

"Save the drama for your mama," was a quote from my late friend, tennis coach, and attorney, Dan Eaton.

Dan would always say this when someone started to complain.

Complaining and gossiping often travel together. Complaining on the outside is a sign you are not healthy on the inside. Many people who feel inferior or inadequate feel the need to put someone or something else down.

My friends, twin brothers Dr. Michael and Dr. David Hughes, were wearing rubber bands on their wrists at a seminar I attended a few years ago. They shared with me, whenever one of them complained, the other would point it out and they had to snap the rubber band, thus causing pain. Before long, they would catch themselves. Eventually, they would stop complaining altogether.

> "Pessimists can usually accurately describe a situation, but optimists are healthier and live longer."
> – Bernie Siegel

I bought an entire box of rubber bands and handed them out to everyone in my life.

To take it a step further, my brother Mike and I had a running bet ... if either one of us spoke any negativity about anyone, we would have to pay the other $50!

Make the decision to eliminate complaining and these other destructive habits from your life. Next time someone starts down this road, just hold up your hand

and say emphatically, "Save the drama for your mama."

Awareness is always the first step. I'm glad this chapter is over; even just writing about these diseases has been a negative experience.

DAY 16
Good or Bad, Hard to Say

We must learn to deal with not always getting what we want.

Have you ever heard, "Don't get your hopes up?"

Well, I prefer to take my chances. I would prefer to still have hope in my life and deal with the occasional letdown.

Even though it is natural to feel disappointment after a setback, we must not let it affect us so much that it affects the big picture. We must not lose our cool.

You can watch this unfold in many different ways:

- A golfer makes a bad shot, then loses his focus for the rest of the round.

- A pitcher gives up a home run and can't seem to regain his composure.

- A tennis player loses momentum after a tough call and begins missing every shot.

- A salesman loses a big sale and can't get out of bed the next day.

- A jilted lover doesn't date for months or years because of a broken heart.

Life is like the seasons. Spring follows winter, every year. Every up must have a down. Every day must have a night.

The quicker your recovery time and your ability to bounce back, the less damage you will do to the overall goal.

We must discipline our disappointments. What do you do to get back on track?

One of my mantras is, "This, too, shall pass." Another is, "Act the way you want to feel and soon you will feel the way that you act."

Realize we all have problems and face setbacks. Stop making it your story. Do not let your failures define you. The more you do, the longer it stays part of your story. Everything is temporary. This, too, shall pass.

You can tell a lot by who you go to for advice when you are upset or suffer a setback. Some friends will commiserate and throw you a pity party. It might sound fun because it's a party, but it's not. Is this really what is best for you?

I don't think so.

Then there are other friends that may say things like "Suck it up, buttercup." This may be a little strong, but sometimes the best medicine is.

If the situation is over and can't be saved, the quicker you move on, the better.

Momentum is a fragile thing, and you need to get back on the horse ASAP.

Remember, you are the author of your life. Take authority. You get to decide when one chapter is over and the next begins. This is even more important as a leader. Your team is watching you and they need you. Be strong for them.

Have you ever been disappointed, only to realize later the incident was a huge blessing in disguise?

There is an old Chinese proverb that goes like this:

> Once, there was a Chinese farmer who worked his poor farm together with his son and their horse. When the horse ran off one day, neighbors came to say, "How unfortunate for you!" The farmer replied, "Good or bad, hard to say."
>
> When the horse returned, followed by a herd of 20 wild horses, the neighbors gathered around and exclaimed, "What good luck for you!" The farmer stayed calm and replied, "Good or bad, hard to say."
>
> While trying to tame one of the wild horses, the farmer's son was violently thrown off and broke his leg. He had to rest up and couldn't help with the farm chores. "How sad for you," the

neighbors cried. "Good or bad, hard to say," said the farmer.

Shortly thereafter, a neighboring army threatened the farmer's village. All the young men in the village were drafted to fight the invaders. Many died. But the farmer's son had been left out of the fighting because of his broken leg. People said to the farmer, "What a good thing your son couldn't fight!" "Good or bad, hard to say," was all the farmer said.

The moral of this story is no event, in and of itself, can truly be judged as good or bad, lucky or unlucky, fortunate or unfortunate, but only time will tell the whole story.

It is best not to get too attached, upset, or disappointed. Many times, it turns out to be the opportunity we have been waiting for, and even praying for, when looked at in hindsight.

So, go with the flow, take things in stride, and remember, "Good or bad, hard to say."

DAY 17
Making $ on Purpose
By Mike Melia

How you view the universe matters. Most of us have grown up in a universe of scarcity. Hence, that is what you hold to be true. If that's you, you have to change that viewpoint if your goal is to manifest abundance.

Ask yourself, "Is the universe a friendly place?"

Be honest with yourself. Your starting point is your starting point. You don't need or really want to impose this view upon yourself, but rather explore the reality of the universe. Explore your own beliefs about money.

> "The most important question you can ever ask is if the world is a friendly place."
> — *Albert Einstein*

Your subconscious mindset was created through your interpretation of life's events over time. One of the practices you can employ to move to a mindset of abundance is to question your current beliefs and assumptions. We are most often unconscious of the conclusions we have drawn about life, yet those "beliefs" held to be true in our subconscious mind create the circumstances of our lives.

Here's an exercise:

> Write down seven ways the universe is an
> unfriendly place. Now, write down seven ways
> the universe is a friendly place. Compare the
> lists and notice the feelings you had while
> writing those things down. Seeing the universe
> as abundant or scarce is a choice. When you
> realize your money mindset is something you've
> adopted, then you also realize you can re-
> design that mindset.

Gratitude Is the Key

Although gratitude is invisible, begin to see it and feel
it as a powerful force. Consciously focus on being
grateful as you walk through the day. Be grateful for
the gift of life.

Look around at your own life and spend more time
and attention on what you are grateful for rather than
what is missing in your life. If you are going through
tough times, don't allow yourself to be resentful. If you
are prone to complaining, STOP!

Practice looking for the good in every situation.

By relentlessly practicing appreciation, the invisible
forces will begin to tip in your favor. As the energy
shifts, be grateful for that. Be grateful for everything
that comes your way, especially small favors and
simple kindnesses.

The most important element of making money on purpose is your mindset. An attitude of gratitude is essential. As you get better and better at practicing appreciation, even in unwanted situations, you will notice more and more good stuff coming your way. Be grateful.

In order to receive the riches you desire, you have to give first. Gratitude and generosity live hand in hand. A grateful person intuitively knows it is through giving that he or she sets it up to receive.

> "Life is a gift from the great spirit. What you do with it is your gift back."
> — Native American saying

Learn to be generous. There are so many things you can give that require nothing other than the desire to be friendly and kind. Give a kind word. Give a helping hand. Smile. Hold a door open for somebody. Practice random acts of kindness.

Money Is Energy

How you *feel* about money will determine your ongoing experience with money. If you feel money is a pain, it will manifest as such. If you don't like money, you will avoid it. On the other hand, if you feel good about money, you will attract it.

When I first got this concept, everything began to change. In his book, *The Trick to Money Is Having Some*, Stuart Wilde advises you (and I agree) to accept all of the money that comes our way, even if it means picking up a penny in a mud puddle on a busy street during rush hour. If you ask the universe for money, accept it.

I began to notice and find money everywhere. And it wasn't just pennies or coins. One day, I found a roll of twenties in New York City, around the corner from where I lived. The idea is to accept what the universe is offering you and not to be too proud, no matter the amount. However, if you find a wallet or any sort of identification, then give the money back. This isn't about claiming what isn't rightfully yours.

Along with opening up to the flow of cash into my life, I also began to open up to new ways of generating cash flow and being more receptive in other areas of my life.

The net effect of being more open is that more energy flows through you. You become more energetic, and also as a result, you become more attractive.

If you combine feeling good about money with being grateful for everything, you are stacking the metaphysical deck in your favor. Add to that a deepening comprehension there is true abundance available, and you will be on your way to becoming an unstoppable force.

Living a Life of Purpose

You may already have a sense of purpose, or maybe you have a feeling there is some kind of purpose you haven't discovered yet.

When you instill a sense of purpose into your money-making activities, you are infusing it with a powerful force. The idea of making money on purpose is very powerful. It really comes down to the idea and practice of living a purposeful life – living a life of conscious choice.

If you haven't discovered your purpose yet, ask yourself what you want your life to be about. What do you love to do? Before you hit your teenage years and were told that there were limits, what were you dreaming of doing or becoming?

Aligning your passions with a career or business is making money on purpose. Statistics show over 75% of people do not enjoy what they do for work every day. That is not living a purposeful life.

"Give me a lever long enough and a fulcrum on which to place it and I shall move the world."
– Archimedes

Here is another powerful exercise. Make a list of all of your values and passions. This could be helping people, traveling, making people laugh, music, etc. Now, one at a time, make a list of all possible occupations or businesses you could do or start while spending time with your passions.

This is what creating your own future is all about. Life flows so much easier and better when you are spending your day doing what you love or what is important to you.

Profits Are Better than Wages

In addition to improving your relationship with money and discovering your purpose, you want to make sure you are buying into the right plan.

"Profits are better than wages," Jim Rohn observed. When we trade our time for money, no matter how much we charge per hour, we are acting as a wage slave and putting a cap on our income.

Leverage manifests as money flowing in without your direct action. If you get paid every time a gizmo you invented or promote gets sold, then you are creating leverage, unless you have to be at the point of sale. This is the difference between linear income and geometric income.

Whatever business enterprise you engage in, continually seek to improve your craft. Continue to seek excellence. Remember, what you send out comes back; as you sow, so shall you reap.

DAY 18
Life Is a Contact Sport

To make our goals and dreams come true, we must make the most out of all our resources. At the top of the list are the people who you know. We have all heard the old saying, "It's not what you know, it's who you know."

I like this better:

It's what you know multiplied by who you know.

Keep in mind, if people don't like you, they won't want to do business with you, and they certainly aren't going to introduce you to their tribe.

Harvey Mackay wrote a book, *Swim with the Sharks Without Being Eaten Alive*. I read this book 25 years ago, and I still remember and use much of it today. Mackay discusses that his most important asset is his Rolodex. As he shared in his 1988 book, we all know 200 people by their first name. So do our 200. That is 40,000 contacts who are one introduction away.

Today, with social media and so many ways to find people, I would put that number around at least 1,000. That means, if your 1,000 know a 1,000, that's one million contacts.

What are you doing to creatively access these folks? You want to provide value and also find a way to stay in touch with them. Harvey's book and system to continue building your rolodex will be a huge asset to you.

It is important whenever you are starting a new project to take some time and make a contact list. Who should go on there? Everyone. Whether they are directly related to your field or project isn't important. Everyone knows someone who knows someone who might be.

So, spend some time looking through all the chapters of your life.

Where have you lived? Make a list.

Write down all of those places. Now, spend time writing down what schools, jobs, businesses, or projects you worked on during each time frame.

For me, it goes like this:

- Born in Bethpage, NY 1970-1978, St. James

- Sebastian, FL 1978-1988, Sebastian Jr Hi, Vero Beach Senior High, Publix Supermarkets, Dodgertown

- St. Augustine, FL 1988-1992, Flagler College

- Columbia, SC 1992-1993, Scentura Creations

- West Orange, NJ 1993-1997, The Zeisler Group, The People's Network

- Atlanta, GA 1997-1999, The People's Network/ Pre-Paid Legal

- Encinitas, CA 2000-2006, PPL

- Wilmington, NC 2006-2015, *162, The Last 42*

- San Diego, CA 2015-2016, The 162 Experience

- Mount Pleasant, SC 2017

Wow, that was an interesting exercise. Continue this exercise by writing an exhaustive list, without pre-judging, of your contacts from each era.

Networking

There are plenty of groups in your area with people who are looking to promote their businesses and hear about whatever you are doing. I recommend trying meet-ups, or even starting your own group that targets exactly the people you are looking to meet.

A few years ago, we created our own networking events to showcase our business. For years, my company would have a 45-minute lunch presentation. Because we were inviting people to come out and listen for our reasons, the attendance was sporadic at best. In fact, most of the time, there were more of our sales people attending than prospects. That's not good.

So, we re-launched the lunches and called them networking events. We began each lunch by encouraging each guest to stand up and give their 45-second commercial.

This accomplished several objectives. People started to show up in droves, because it was about them, not us.

When I moved to Wilmington, North Carolina in 2006, we hosted one of these lunches within 30 days of moving to town, knowing no one. We had 40 local professionals show up. Some of the people there that day have helped us grow our business tremendously and have been a resource since.

We made the invitation fairly simple. "Do you like to network? I am sponsoring an event for 30-35 local professionals, business people, and community leaders. Everyone gets 45 seconds to do their commercial or introduce themselves. Does that sound like something you may be interested in?"

We simply became the sponsors of these events and just wanted to be known as great networkers who connected local business people. People do business with people they know, like, and trust.

Our cost of doing the event went down to virtually nothing, because all of the networkers were now buying their own lunch, and they were now helping us do the inviting/marketing.

We also quickly realized we could say everything we needed to in just 12 minutes. They left wanting to learn more, not feeling like they were sold.

We eventually added another speaker to each event and gave them a ten-minute spot. We have been able to spread these "networking events" throughout the US and Canada and have grown our business substantially in the process.

How to Win Friends and Influence People

Since you are going through all of the trouble of meeting people and re-connecting with those from the past, you might as well make the most out of it.

Dale Carnegie's *How to Win Friends and Influence People* may be one of the best books ever written on the topic of human interaction.

If you are in the people business at any level, which should be all of us, this classic is a must read.

Let's review a few of Carnegie's key points before going out to network.

#1 – Make sure to be a good listener.

This means you genuinely care about what the other person is talking about. Put your needs to talk about yourself, your business, or product aside. If they like you, they will want to know about you later. They will want to do business with you.

#2 – Encourage others to talk about themselves.

People love to tell their story. Everyone is tuned into their favorite radio station, WIIFM. (What's in it for me?) Be different and let them talk. The less you talk, the more fascinating they will think you are. As Carnegie teaches, "Be interested, not interesting."

#3 – Make others feel important.

You do this by not only being an active listener, but by truly being interested in what they have to say. Ask questions. Ask how they arrived in their field, or even better, what a good referral would be. Pretend they have a flashing sign on their head that reads, "Make me feel special."

#4 – Remember their names.

You will most likely see these people again at another networking event. You will score some huge points by remembering their names and recalling something they spoke of last time.

If you are one of those people who say, "I'm just not that good at remembering names."

Stop it.

You know that is an excuse and can be fixed by focusing more on the other person than on yourself. No one was born with the skill of remembering names. It's developed, just like everything else.

If you are unsure if you have met them before, say, "it is nice to see you," rather than, "it is nice to meet you."

Introduce them to others at networking events using the same commercial they just gave you. People can be shy at these types of events and they will appreciate having you as an ally.

#5 – Don't criticize, condemn, or complain.

Networkers love to talk. Don't get the reputation of being a Debbie Downer. Also, make sure to avoid any controversial topics, like politics and religion. This is the fastest way to lose a friend or potential client. And never correct anyone else in public or in front of their peers, even if you know they are wrong. Bite your tongue and let them save face.

Always be focused on opening new doors, meeting new people, and even living in new places. In *Be Obsessed or Be Average*, modern day business philosopher Grant Cardone shares his strategies on this topic. He urges his readers to consider moving to places they have never lived to force themselves out of their comfort zone and meet new people.

> "I've learned that people will forget what you said, people will forget what you did, but people will never forget how you made them feel."
> – *Maya Angelou*

In *Titans* by Tim Ferris, he talks about developing 1,000 super fans. These are the people who love you and your work so much, they will buy everything you come out with. 1,000 seems much more manageable than 1,000,000.

You must find a way to communicate regularly with this group and give them some level of a personal touch. Let's say you produce a product, good, or service. If the average member of your tribe spends $100 per year, there is your 6-figure income.

To reach new levels in your life, you must meet new people and always be building a better team. The team that has gotten you to where you are won't be the same team to help get you to the next level.

Be willing to spread your wings and fulfill your purpose by developing and nurturing your contact list.

DAY 19

Success Is a Numbers Game

Success takes time, 10,000 hours to be exact! In Malcolm Gladwell's book, *Outliers*, he does an entire chapter on the principle of 10,000 hours. He uses many examples of how it takes roughly 10,000 hours to master your craft. Whether it is Bill Gates learning about computers, the Beatles jamming for eight hours a day, or the Williams sisters picking up rackets before they could walk, champions put in their time.

They lose themselves for hours because they love what they do. Have you discovered, as we discussed on Day 17, what your passions are? It's hard to put in 10,000 hours if you don't absolutely love it.

Do the math and give yourself some time. 40 hours per week multiplied by 50 weeks annually is 2,000 hours. So, let's say it will take five years of a full-time, all-in study and practice of your craft effort to be among the elite in your field.

Will the juice be worth the squeeze? Will there be gold at the end of the rainbow? Do you know others in your field who are amongst the best? Have they achieved the results and lifestyle from their fanatical effort? If you are going to take the time, energy, and massive action necessary, you'll want to make sure your ladder is up against the right wall.

Many times, we hear success stories of what seems like overnight success, but in truth, there is always a story behind the story.

In our own journey of network marketing, Mike and I had worked full-time from November of 1994 through September of 1998. It was almost four solid years of intense effort, while we often struggled financially. There were two of us, and we built a fairly large team. I would say that we were on a fast-paced course for our 10,000 hours.

We joined our current company on October 1st, and in our first three months, earned over $68,000. We had never earned this kind of income, and everyone around us thought we were having instant success. The reality is, we worked like crazy for four years.

If you want to get paid for more than your worth, you must first do more than you get paid for.

80/20 Rule

Another formula I follow is the 80/20 rule. There are a lot of different ways to look at this. 80% of our results come from 20% of our efforts, or if you lead a team, the top 20% of your people.

So, pinpoint what activities (20%) bring you in the most money or results and do that as much as you can (80% of the time.)

Jim Rohn calls these majors (20%) and minors (80%). Don't major in the minors. Spend 80% of your time doing the top 20% payoff activity.

In the same light, spend 80% of your time with the 20% of leaders in your organization who get the biggest results. If you run a team, the top 20% get your personal one-on-one time, and everyone else gets group time. This might be conference calls, sales meetings, etc. Make the 80% earn your personal time.

Know Your Numbers

When you do something often enough, ratios begin to appear. If you are in sales, how many people on average must you speak with to get an appointment?

How many appointments do you average before you get a "YES?"

Let's say your commission is $100. Your average reflects that 1/2 of the people will give you an appointment. You must contact 20 to get 10 appointments. Of the 10 appointments, five buy. So, let's say your goal is to earn $1000 this week. You need 10 to buy, which means you need 20 presentations, meaning you need to ask 40 for an appointment. This means you are averaging $25 per phone call and $50 per appointment.

So, you can make more money by contacting more prospects, improving your ratios, and getting better at setting appointments. Your presentation will get better over time as well.

Take Inventory

It is hard to reach a goal if you do not know where your starting point is. Whether you own a retail store or run a sales team, it is important to inspect what you expect.

This means every business or project should have numbers you will want to constantly monitor, so you will know whether you are winning or losing. Whether you are on track or off track.

Think about a Las Vegas Casino. They are constantly adding up whether a specific table is up or down. Some numbers cannot wait until the end of the day to take a look at. It could be too late.

Know your most important numbers and keep an eye on them.

DAY 20

Failing to Plan Is Planning to Fail

Extraordinary results don't happen by accident. In his book *21 Irrefutable Laws of Leadership,* John Maxwell explains one leadership attribute is The Law of Navigation. A great leader has the ability to look ahead and plan for pitfalls or landmines and anticipate potential challenges.

Sometimes, you might call this person a control freak. I'm glad to report that I've been called this myself. Well, these over planners are more likely to get the job done if they think of everything.

Here's the truth:

Proper Planning Prevents Poor Performance

To Do Lists

It is important you finish things first on paper and make lists of things that need to be done. When I set out to break my own record of attending 176 straight NY Yankee games, I had a list of over 60 things that needed to be done.

Also, make sure to identify obstacles. For those who read my first book, *162 The Almost Epic Journey of A*

Yankee Superfan, you may remember that I laid out all possible obstacles I might face in the first chapter.

Next, make a list of all the people who could serve as resources. For me, it was media contacts, comedy contacts, law firms with season tickets, friends who live in all of the American league cities, possible sponsors, etc.

Make sure to identify the skills, knowledge, and education you will need to achieve your goals. As with everything you plan, the more specific, the better.

Prioritize

After you have a complete list, organize and prioritize the list. Use the 80/20 rule to decide what to do first. Out of every ten items, what one or two are the most important? When you start working the lists, it becomes obvious what needs to be done and what would simply be nice.

List, in sequence, every single step you will need to take. Steven Covey, in *Seven Habits of Highly Effective People,* reminds us to begin with the end in mind. Visualize the result you want and work backwards. Set your own personal deadlines. This will keep you on track.

> "Every minute spent in planning saves you 10 minutes in execution."
> – Brian Tracy

Once you have your list prioritized by importance, you have your check list.

Plan Each Day the Evening Before

Let your subconscious mind have the night to come up with creative ideas. Have you ever woken up in the middle of the night with an idea? This is your friend, the subconscious mind, doing their part.

Start/Complete Your Most Important Task

It is important to complete one thing at a time before you move on. This is called single-handling. Start and don't move on until you've completed that single project. Your confidence will grow with every completed item. Remember to start with the most important item.

Plan-Do-Review

The best time to evaluate how something went is right after its completion, while everything is fresh in your mind. You plan it, you do it, and then you immediately review it.

Ask yourself and your team, what worked? What didn't work? If you want to get better, don't be attached to your ego and accept the feedback. This is no time to be sensitive.

When you are in a leadership position, make sure to give constructive feedback to those you are training.

First, let them know what they did right. Always praise before teaching. Most of the time, people know what they did wrong. There is no need to make them feel worse.

Ask questions rather than just pointing it out. How did you think that went? How do you think we could have improved our outcome for next time? What lessons did you learn? If they did make mistakes, let them know, if applicable, that you once made the same mistakes and what you did to correct them.

> "The time to prepare isn't after you have been given the opportunity. It's long before that opportunity arises. Once the opportunity arrives, it's too late to prepare."
> – John Wooden

People know when they mess up and feel badly enough. Make sure to end on a high note. My good friend and mentor, Jeff Bell, refers to this as the sandwich technique … praise-teach-praise.

An important part of goal-achieving is the planning process. The plan you start with isn't the plan you'll end with. Be flexible.

Practice, Practice, Practice

Lastly, one of the best things you can do to best prepare is to practice. Luck is when preparedness meets opportunity. If you met the perfect person today to help complete your goal, would you be ready? Are you currently at the top of your game?

Let's pretend that you are a stand-up comic. If The Tonight Show called, do you have your five minutes ready to go tomorrow night?

Michael Jordan was always the first and last one at the gym. Was he practicing because everyone else was better than him? No, he was better than everyone else because he practiced. He was always prepared.

It's Still Rock and Roll to Me

In the eighth grade, Liberty Devitto saw the Beatles perform on the Ed Sullivan show. He knew immediately he wanted to play the drums in a rock and roll band. He practiced non-stop. You never know when the call is going to come.

"I graduated high school in 1968 and that was in June. In November, I get a phone call from Billy Joel. 'Hey, our drummer got sick and we need a drummer.'"

Devitto replied, "When?"

"Tonight."

> "Practice isn't the thing you do once you are good. It's the thing that you do that makes you good."
> – Malcolm Gladwell

Devitto went to work as Joel's drummer for nearly three decades. What most people don't know is Devitto was not the first phone call Billy Joel made that day, but he was the first one to be ready.

Be ready when your call comes.

DAY 21

Don't Quit

Once you have decided what you want and you begin your journey, there will be many ups and downs. Persistency will be a key to your success. Many of the 30 ways in this book will help you hold it together.

Having clearly defined goals, a supportive network, and a steady diet of personal development will certainly help. You need a strategy, though. A resilience.

What will you do when the going gets tough?

The poem *Don't Quit* was taped on our closet door in our war room (bedroom). We read it out aloud with enthusiasm whenever the need arose.

Don't Quit

When things go wrong, as they sometimes will,
When the road you're trudging seems all uphill,
When the funds are low and the debts are high,
And you want to smile, but you have to sigh,

When care is pressing you down a bit –
Rest if you must, but don't you quit.
Life is queer with its twists and turns,

As every one of us sometimes learns,
And many a fellow turns about
When he might have won had he stuck it out.

Don't give up though the pace seems slow –
You may succeed with another blow.
Often the goal is nearer than
It seems to a faint and faltering man;
Often the struggler has given up
When he might have captured the victor's cup;
And he learned too late when the night came down,
How close he was to the golden crown.

Success is failure turned inside out –
The silver tint in the clouds of doubt,
And you never can tell how close you are,
It might be near when it seems afar;
So, stick to the fight when you're hardest hit –
It's when things seem worst that you must not quit.

Persistence is self-discipline in action. Your willingness to persist when things go wrong or when you encounter obstacles is a sign of your character and your self-confidence goes up every time you persist. Our character is revealed, not when things go right, but when we face adversity.

Remember, most people quit. Decide early on you won't be one of them.

Or Maybe You Should Quit

You got to know when to hold em'
Know when to fold em'
Know when to walk away
and know when to run.
  — *The Gambler*, Kenny Rogers

You also have to be able to identify times when you should quit. If a business, project, or person is no longer serving your greater vision, you must have the intuition and courage to pick up your stakes and move on. This is when it's useful to have a coach or mentor who will have your best interests in mind.

> Our character is revealed, not when things go right, but when we face adversity.

Some of my best decisions have been when I knew it was time to walk away. Others have been when I've stuck it out.

Don't quit because something is harder than you thought. This just means you need to get better. You need to develop the skills over time.

Quit because you realize this is no longer your best path. Stay true to yourself and your values.

I learned a technique early in my career. When someone wanted to quit my team, I would sit them down and ask, "Why did you originally start with us?"

They would share their reason with me. It was usually very personal and often profound.

"What about that has changed?"

Inevitably, they would respond by saying, "Nothing." Their need still existed.

After further discussion, we often agreed what had changed was how hard sales was, and they felt discouraged.

I would let them know I also wanted to give up many times, and what they were experiencing was natural and to be expected. I would challenge them to get better.

Yeah, You Should Quit

We all have bad, destructive, and even dangerous habits we know aren't serving us. Put it this way, if whatever you are doing has groups of people who meet on a regular basis with the word anonymous after it, it's probably slowing you down. None of us want to believe we have challenges or addictions, but we do. The sooner you cut these things out of your life, the better.

I had a problem with sports betting for a time. I knew it was a problem because I would hide it from certain people. Another reason was because I would lose more than I won. Also, it was stealing some of my mental energy and focus I could have used for other goals.

So, one day, I just quit. It was a great decision. Whatever it is I made you think of as you read these last few paragraphs, you may want to consider quitting.

Always remember to replace a bad habit with a new, good one. Things can be easier to quit if you have something new and positive to focus on.

DAY 22

Know the Game You Are In

Many of the 30 ways have been focused on becoming the best you can be. We have discussed getting a coach and also reading and listening to inspirational and educational information as part of your daily regimen.

Many people not only change jobs often, but are now changing careers every few years. Every industry has its benefits, drawbacks, and nuances.

Picking the right field can be tricky, especially with the speed of technology and how fast things are changing.

Jobs of 10 and 20 years ago may now be totally obsolete.

If you want to increase your earning power, pick an industry and master it. Know the game you are in. Decide to have a career rather than a job. Put in your 10,000 hours.

It is first important to ask if you believe you are in the right industry.

Many times, we find ourselves in a career because we had a friend or neighbor or some circumstance that introduced us, and it is not really where we want to be or where we are best suited. So, first we must examine and ask ourselves:

Why do I do what I do?

Take a few moments and mull this over and list all the benefits that you receive. What do you like most about it? If you had to start over, would you be doing the same thing? Is this really what you want to be doing?

Is your current career part of your master plan? If you become one of the best in your industry, will you achieve the level of freedom or success you desire?

At some point, will you be able to walk away with your income still intact or possibly transition to something that would fit your lifestyle as you grow older?

I chose network marketing to be the industry I mastered. I often joke that some, depending on their experience, swear by it and others swear at it. This has been my industry for the last 25 years.

Here are a few of my reasons:

- There are thousands of people in my industry who make substantial incomes of over a million dollars per year. In meeting many of them, it is obvious most are very ordinary, which gave me hope.

- What is uncommon about most of their success is they do not have to work anymore, and if they do, it is mostly just giving speeches and meeting people at social events.

- I really didn't see any other opportunity that would give me both the financial and the time freedom to go along with it. In short, it was the leveraged income of team building that attracted me.

- It has enabled me to start a part-time stand-up comedy business. I have also had the opportunity to take some time off and follow my passion for the NY Yankees, and have discovered I love to write books. The time freedom also allowed my family to launch and support our foundation, Work Play Love.

> "Find something you love to do and you'll never have to work a day in your life."
> — Harvey Mackay

- I really enjoy the quality and diversity of the people I have met along the way. Because of the nature of the business, I have come to enjoy many strong relationships. That wasn't necessarily why I joined, but it is one of the benefits.

- I love the teamwork aspect of helping others achieve their goals and change their lives. It keeps me inspired.

- I prefer to work from home, with no boss, and I also love to travel to exotic destinations around the world.

- I enjoy the personal development and continuous environment of success network marketing offers. I like the competitive environment and appreciate the recognition that accompanies success.

- Lastly, I feel good when I share our service with others and truly believe my empowered customers are the biggest winners.

This was a good exercise for me to do along with you, as it helped me revisit why I do what I do.

Now let's take a look at the cons.

- I am in a highly scrutinized profession. Most people I know outside of my field do not really understand what I do. Some even call it a pyramid, or say that I'm in "one of those things." Even though that comes from a lack of understanding, it can still be hurtful when people judge without any real knowledge.

- We also have fairly high turnover. As in many other industries, we have people who see the potential and get started, but do not follow through and do the work and wind up quitting. That can be frustrating, and I don't like to see others fail when I know they have tons of potential.

- It is hard when you first get started. Building and running a "volunteer army" takes effort, time, and patience. During the beginning of my career, I had to sacrifice and attend functions when I wasn't making any money. Sometimes these were on Saturdays or at night, when my friends were inviting me to do something more fun.

- Another drawback might be that I have seen a lot of people think the grass is greener and jump around from company to company, always looking for the right deal. This can give our industry a bad name or the perception that we are always trying to sell people something.

> "If you read ten pages a day pertaining to your field, you would be in the top ten percent of your field in five years."
> – Brian Tracy

I tried to list as many things as possible and tried to not sound like a commercial for my industry, but you know what...

I LOVE WHAT I DO!

Before you go all in, decide if you are where you want to be. Weigh your pros and cons and decide for yourself.

If you don't think you are in the right industry for you, the sooner you make a move, the better.

Be Coachable

Decide to master your industry. You want to be so hungry, you are always the most coachable person in the room.

Let's look at the path to mastery.

Learned Knowledge

This is the classroom, books, and anything you can go study. What are the best ten books in your industry and how successful are the people who wrote them? Consume them.

Turn your car into a rolling university. We spend an average of over 500 hours per year in our cars. Invest this "downtime" in learning everything you can from audios and podcasts. In *The 162 Experience*, I interview some of the most successful people in business, sports, and life, so you, me, and others can learn and improve.

Activity Knowledge

We gain the most insight from putting what we learn into action right away. As scary as this might seem, you must jump in and try things for yourself. For those of us who have ever been in sales, we can probably remember the terror that accompanied our first sales call or presentation.

We must get out of the classroom and put our knowledge to work. Don't be afraid to make mistakes. Just be sure to learn from them as much as possible.

Modeling Knowledge

Every great team has veterans you can learn from. One of my roles with my company today is to serve as a mentor and friend to the next generation. I love this and enjoy offering my expertise to those who desire success.

Chances are, you can find someone like this in your field. Ask and ye shall find. These folks have made the mistakes and have widened the path. Find a mentor worth following.

> "While some people are studying the roots, others are picking the fruit. It just depends on which end of this you want to get in on."
> – Jim Rohn

Teaching Knowledge

If you want to make a little money, learn your business.

If you want to make more money, teach others what you've learned.

If you want to make the big money, teach others to teach what you've learned. In other words, lead the leaders. Coach the coaches.

We learn the most when we must think, formulate, and communicate our experiences with others, and that happens when we teach.

Have you ever had to train a new employee or a team? You probably put in more effort to learn the material than any other time, because you wanted to get it right and prove you knew your material.

Become Part of the 1%

The bottom line, folks, is the competition is not that tough. First, become part of the top 20% by showing up consistently and outworking everyone around you. Based on your other experiences, this may happen right away or could take several years. If you feel your peers are excelling more quickly than you, remember there is always a story behind the story. Everyone pays their dues at some point.

> "Eighty percent of success is showing up."
> – Woody Allen

Separate yourself a second time and join the top 20% of the top 20%, by studying your field, goal-setting, and absorbing these 30 ways. This will put you in the top 4%. You are well on your way to mastering your craft and are probably getting close to your 10,000 hours.

That's a good start. You are probably getting results or making a good living at this point. Don't get too comfortable or rest on your laurels. This is where many slow down, because their needs are being met. They become satisfied.

Now, look around and out-work, out-study and out-perform your peers and join the top 20% of the top 4%. You are now in the top .08% of your field.

Congratulations, you should be able to write your own ticket. This might take 10-15 years, but you are going to be 10-15 years older anyway, right?

Success is easy, just separate yourself from the competition three times.

DAY 23

Use Your Imagination

Let me start Day 23 by saying I a firm believer, when it comes to your core business, in having a system and sticking with it.

The acronym for S.Y.S.T.E.M. is save yourself some time, energy, and money. I've been heard hundreds of times, preaching not to re-invent the wheel.

Yesterday we talked about knowing the game you are in. In all industries, there are tried and true methods of success. Don't deviate from what works. What I'm about to discuss is in addition to staying within your system. You are not brainstorming to avoid this, but to enhance it.

It only takes one good idea to jump start a business, attract a whole new client base, or change your life.

Today we are going to do an exercise in thinking outside the box called "mindstorming." I learned this at a Brian Tracy seminar and use this approach often. It is a game-changer.

You have all the inner resources available to you in your own head. You are a creative human being. Thoughts are things. Every great idea starts as just that, an idea.

You can improve your imagination by using it. Today we are going to take your mind to the gym for a workout. The more you use it, the more powerful you and your ideas will become. It only takes one.

Ask a focused question. What one problem, if you were to solve it, would have the greatest positive impact on your business or your life? Or what one goal, if achieved, would have the greatest impact on your sales or profitability?

> "A mind is like a parachute. It doesn't work if it is not open."
> – Frank Zappa

Grab a notebook and lock yourself away from any distractions. If you have a workout or mastermind partner who shares your goal, include him or her.

Choose that problem or goal and write a question at the top of the page.

For instance:

> How can I sell 25,000 copies of my book in 90 days?

> How can we raise $100,000 for our charity this year?

Now, write down 20 answers you haven't thought of before. There are no wrong answers. Allow your creative juices to flow. This may be difficult at the beginning, much like hitting the weights after a long break. The most unique ideas usually come toward the end of the list. Go past 20 if they are flowing. If you are doing this with a partner, do not judge the other's ideas. Just write them down. Judging stymies your creativity.

Please don't go to Day 24 until you have completed this task.

You got this.

Great! How did that feel? Go through your list and select one idea and implement it right away. The sooner you implement it, the more effective it will be.

DAY 24

Be Accountable

In day one we discussed writing down your wins from the previous 24 hours. This is a good start. You should also end every day by writing down what you did today to move one of your most important goals forward. If everyone on the team did what you did today, are you ok with that?

Who do you answer to?

At the end of the day, you are the most important person who needs to be accountable. Do not let yourself slide, or off the hook.

Remember, commitment is doing the thing you said you would do after the feeling you said it with has left you. If that inspired feeling has left you temporarily, who is going to be there to urge you to keep going?

Workout Partner

Having a workout partner is key to your success. We all need someone who is experiencing what we are to talk to on a regular basis and keep us in check. The best way to find a great workout partner is to be one.

Write down all the qualities you'd like in a partner. Ask yourself, would someone be lucky to have you as a partner? Are you willing to encourage someone when they need it? Will you push someone when they don't feel like taking action?

Ask them upfront, what has stopped them in the past? Ask for permission to coach when they need it. Give them permission to coach you.

When selecting your workout partner, find someone who is at least as ambitious as you and is committed to their own success. Do not pick someone who is a complainer or negative in any capacity.

This will have the opposite effect of what you are looking for. I recommend you have a trial period for being workout partners. Try it out for a week or so and make sure it is a good fit for both of you. This should be a motivating experience, not a draining one.

Mastermind Group

Whether it is a workout partner, a coach, or a mastermind group, someone besides you needs to have input.

The power of a mastermind is that it creates a third, more powerful mind. Having someone else creates synergy. Mastermind groups are a larger version of having a workout partner, in which you can draw from more than one person's experiences. These groups meet on a regular basis and may or may not share common goals.

Although you might not be in the same industry or be working on the same projects, a mastermind group can provide many different outlooks and perspectives. These groups can be an enormous asset in coming up with new ideas, providing resources, and staying accountable.

You should have a daily, weekly, monthly, quarterly, and annual plan-do-review of your goals and progress. You can do this by yourself or with your partners.

> "If it is to be, it is up to me."
> – William H. Johnsen

By setting goals regularly, you should be getting immediate feedback on how you are doing. Are you hitting your goals? Why or why not?

Let's take a look at some of your goals. Pick a health goal. Would you be better off if you were spending time with someone who had that same goal? You may exercise together. You would talk about what foods and nutritional choices you are making. You would be way more likely to keep those promises to yourself if someone was sharing the same goal.

Stay with that same health goal. Let's assume you joined a mastermind group such as Weight Watchers. If you had to do a weigh-in every week at the same time, would it make you act differently throughout the week knowing you were going to have to be accountable?

DAY 25
No Problem, Mon

Congrats on making it to Day 25. If you have made it this far, you have a goal and you are on the quest to achieve it. Although this topic is similar to disciplining your disappointments, I wanted to give problem-solving its own day.

No Problem

Let's start by eliminating the word "problem" from our vocabulary. Will that really make that big of a difference? I think so. It adds a lot of unnecessary negative energy to the situation.

Many people who seem to be looking for advice will open up a conversation with, "You know what my problem is?"

Yes, I think to myself, it's your attitude. Let's replace "problem" with the word "challenge." People love a challenge.

If you only experience smooth sailing, I can promise you your goal isn't big enough.

The bigger the goal, the bigger the prize. The bigger the prize, the bigger the sacrifice. The bigger the prize, the more skills you will need to develop. The bigger the prize, the more challenges you will face, and the bigger the leader you will need to become.

The size of a leader is determined by the size of a problem they can overcome.

Every Level Has Its Devil

Anticipate that the path will not be easy. Know in advance, you will have to deal with some tough issues. This is a sign you are growing and reaching new heights. This is great news. You are getting closer to your ultimate goal.

As Jim Rohn used to say, "It's not what you get, it's who you become, and who you become will determine what you get." That is so true!

> "God doesn't give big battles to small soldiers."
> – Tiffany Malott

In all of the 30 ways, I sprinkle in personal development. A great reason to be doing all of this work on yourself is to be prepared for the inevitable challenges. A small leader can be knocked out of the game by a small challenge.

A great leader doesn't lose a lot of sleep or time away from their main focus when challenges arise. They persist with a sense of urgency. They handle it and move on quickly. Even if they take the inevitable step backwards, they keep their eyes on the prize.

"Response" Ability

Do your best to take the emotions out of it and treat everyone involved with respect. "Losing it" can show your lack of emotional intelligence. Nobody wants to be around a hot head. Handling things calmly will say a lot about you.

Steven Covey shares the idea in 7 *Habits of Highly Effective People;* we have the ability to respond to a situation any way we like. There is a moment between a situation and our response. This is the moment of decision.

> "You measure the size of the accomplishment, by the obstacles you had to overcome to reach your goals."
> – Booker T. Washington

Have you ever heard someone say, "They made me angry?" Well, there was whatever happened, and then the decision to be angry or not to be angry. We all have the ability to respond to our choosing. I recommend you take full responsibility for everything that happens to you – whether it is good, bad, or indifferent. It is empowering to know you have caused whatever you are dealing with. That means you can cause a different outcome, and you, and only you, are ultimately responsible for your success or your failure.

I often do speaking engagements. Every so often, the attendance, which is very important, is lacking. I could blame the local promoters who have brought me in. Or I could point at the weather, the current economic trends, or competing events. Or I could look in the mirror and ask, what could I have done differently? What have I done to cause this? What am I attracting?

Blame is the opposite of personal responsibility. It is the ultimate excuse maker. When challenges arise, there is no need to blame. Ask yourself, what will I do next time to avoid the same situation?

The higher you go, the more responsibility you will have. Whether you become a first-time parent or a CEO, the more you are given, the more responsible you'll need to be. Embrace it.

Be willing to be flexible. Be willing to admit when you've been wrong or have made a mistake.

> "When all that we see are problems around us, it means we do not have a clear, specific goal in our vision."
> – Paul J. Meyer

A small leader can be derailed for days or weeks and lose all of their momentum.

Ask yourself, "Can I do anything about this?" If not, why bother getting frustrated? Chalk it up and say, "Good or bad, Hard to say."

If you can do something about it, great. Before you go asking for help, make sure you have fully researched the challenge yourself and make a list of possible solutions. Ask yourself, what outcome do I want to see here?

The Bigger the Test, the Better the Testimonial

I'm proud to say I have been running the same business for nearly 25 years. We have faced a lot of challenges and have stood the test of time. What doesn't kill you will make you stronger. I remember so many different instances on my own personal journey to success in which I turned to Mike and said, *"This will make a great part of the story."*

> "Every adversity, every failure, every heartache carries with it the seed of an equal or greater benefit."
> – Napoleon Hill

I gave my acceptance speech hundreds and hundreds of times in the shower or in the car. In every speech, it was the adversity and hardships that made the story even greater.

I vividly remember sitting on the back porch of my sister's house in West Orange, NJ, where we were living rent-free. Mike and I were sitting with a stack of bills and a fraction of the money, deciding who gets paid that month. That can be a scary and overwhelming experience, if you let it. We would remind each other, this is where most people would quit.

We would have fun with it. I would call back bill collectors and lighten the mood. "It's your lucky day," I would profess, "Your bill has made it to the top of my pile. I am prepared to offer you 40% of what I owe right now. If you decline, I will have to move to the next in line and offer them your money."

If they would hassle me, I would remind them I didn't borrow or owe the money directly to them and they should take it easy.

My favorite move was a time when I mailed the utilities bill to the phone company and the phone bill with a check to the utility company. That trick bought me another week or two.

Nicely played, sir! (But I'm not recommending you do it.)

Stress is a decision. It's not required.

After all, as John Addison says, "Don't take yourself and life too seriously, because no one else does."

DAY 26
Pay Full Retail

Here is an excerpt from *Success Principles*, by Jack Canfield:

> "Behind every great achievement is a story of education, training, practice, discipline, and sacrifice. You have to be willing to pay the price. Maybe that price is pursuing one activity while putting everything else in your life on hold. Maybe it is investing all of your personal wealth or savings. Maybe it's willing to walk away from the safety of your current situation."

How true is that!

Faith and Belief

It takes faith and belief in yourself and in the process.

Why start a race you don't believe you can finish? We must expect that, if we do certain things or, just as importantly, give up certain things, it will work out. In *Think and Grow Rich*, Napoleon Hill shares how the qualities of strong faith and unwavering belief are crucial for success.

I remember sitting in a restaurant with Darren Hardy, the author of *The Compound Effect*, at age 23. We were having breakfast with a small group of entrepreneurs in lower Manhattan. He compared success to a swinging pendulum.

He held both hands up, a few inches apart, clenching his fists. He shook his left hand and said it represented massive success. The right one represented sacrifice, and like a pendulum, one side would only go as far as the other. If you wanted a little success, you made little sacrifices. If you wanted massive success, you made massive sacrifices. I knew that day, I was going to the top. That visual has stayed with me all these years, as every day we are faced with hundreds of choices.

> "All you can do, is all that you can do, but all you can do is enough."
> – Art Williams

The willingness is the magic, though. You have to pay enthusiastically. In fact, the more excited you are about your goal, the less it will seem like work. The willingness will help you persevere when the going gets tough.

For Mike and I, living at our sister's house for years was a sacrifice some wouldn't be willing to make.

Don't get me wrong, our sister Mary couldn't have been more gracious and our accommodations were awesome. But, two male adults sharing the attic room with one queen size bed can humble you.

Your ego or sense of self can take a hit if you let it. We knew we were building something special. We knew our efforts were not in vain. We believed we were going to the top of the mountain or we were going to die on the side, but we weren't going back.

Find Out the Cost

It is one thing to say, "I'll do anything to be successful." It is another to know what you are saying yes to.

The first step is to do some investigating and look further into what is required to reach your goal. You may find the price is too steep. Make a list of those who have accomplished what you want and interview and study them to see if it is worth it. Whether it's the long hours, the toll on your health, or time away from your family, everything has a price. Know what you are agreeing to.

"You have to give up to go up."
– John Maxwell

So, make a list of all the things you are going to have to sacrifice or be willing to do to reach your goal. Make sure to include the long hours, the new skills that will have to be developed, the events you'll have to miss, the comfort zone you'll say goodbye to, and anything else you'll have to forfeit along the way.

For me personally, I viewed every sacrifice as a step on the ladder to success. Every small step was reassurance that I was all in. Every hour was an investment into building the kind of life I was looking for. I wanted time and financial freedom. I was willing to pay for it.

The irony about getting what you want is that you have to give up some of what you already have. You want more time freedom, you must give up some time. You want to make money, you must invest some. You want to be great at something, you must be willing to be bad at it first.

> "Be willing to step up to the counter of success and pay full retail."
> – Brian Carruthers

Have I scared you away yet? I hope not, because every minute has been worth it. I hope you'll find your passion and commit to yourself that you are going all the way.

Huddle Up

Knowing your "why" and what it will take to accomplish your goals can help you on your journey, especially if your "why" is big enough and includes other people. For those who are doing this for their parents, kids, or mate, this can add another level of commitment. We are more likely to quit on ourselves, but not on those who are counting on us the most.

It is important to get the family and those closest to you together and talk about the sacrifices that will be demanded. I suggest a family meeting. Make sure to share with them the rewards as well as the sacrifices.

Imagine the early mornings of an Olympic athlete, the seven months away from the family for an MLB player, or the public life of a politician. Many sacrifices will also be made by those closest to you.

It is best to get their buy-in. Although the road made be a long one, having them understand why you are doing what you are doing and the end game is important.

Whatever It Takes

I love this Jim Rohn quote because it lays it all out there:

> "We must all suffer from one of two pains: the pain of discipline or the pain of regret. The difference is discipline weighs ounces while regret weighs tons."

So, what will it be, winning or losing? You decide.

You must have the whatever-it-takes attitude. Every great success story has examples of disappointments, setbacks, grueling hours, unfavorable opinions from others, and just overall hardship.

Can you handle it?

Do you want it bad enough?

The good news is, you get to decide when enough is enough or if you should keep moving forward. No one can quit for you. You get to write the ending to your story. Remember, you are the author of your life. Make it a great story.

Time Will Promote or Expose You

Too many times I see people weighing how long they have been after their goal and continually judging and contemplating whether it is working.

The challenge with this is that they are continually taking their eyes off of the prize, thus diminishing their life spirit and prolonging the journey, and thus the sacrifice.

Don't look for a shortcut. You are closer than you think. You got this.

DAY 27

Serve the Masses

If you had to boil down your mission statement to just one phrase or sentence, what would it be?

Here's mine:

> To inspire people through my books, talks, podcast, message, and example to live their dreams.

Nothing is more rewarding than someone contacting me and letting me know I made a difference in their life by encouraging them to think or act bigger toward accomplishing a goal.

The great Zig Ziglar famously instructed:

> "Help enough other people get what they want and you can have everything that you want."

Zig encourages us to take the focus off of ourselves and to put it on helping others.

Jim Rohn echoed that point his own way:

> "Service to many leads to fortune."

I come from a competitive field. To excel, one must be goal-oriented and focused. To massively excel, one must help others be goal-oriented and focused. You can still win big when you help others win. In fact, you can win much bigger.

Consider this:

> Success is reaching a pre-determined goal; significance is helping others reach theirs.

It does start with you. The best way to help someone is to be a great example. A great leader leads. A boss tells someone what to do. A great leader shows them what to do and inspires them to do it. Always be willing to do what you are asking others to do.

Whether you are coaching someone on your team or negotiating a business deal, simply ask yourself, what does this other person want? What will make them happy?

> "People don't care how much you know, until they know how much that you care."
> – Theodore Roosevelt

All relationships must be a win/win or they will be doomed. Both parties must feel like they are getting what they want. So, as you are bringing your ideas and goals out to the world, remember people do business with people that they know, like, and trust.

Earn that trust by seeing things from their perspective and doing what you say you'll do.

> "Seek first to understand and then be understood."
> – Stephen Covey

Be willing to help and serve people, whether it has a direct bearing on your goals or not.

As you sow, so shall you reap. Everything comes full circle.

Karma is a beautiful thing when it is on your side. You never know when you'll need it.

Go out and make the world a better place today.

DAY 28

How You Do Anything Is How You Do Everything

We are constantly making decisions throughout the course of our day which ultimately shape our lives. Every choice, no matter how big or small, along with how we make those choices and how we treat others, makes up our overall character.

The "hows" of success are easy. It's how we do the "hows" that makes all the difference.

Do You Brighten a Room or Dim It?

When you walk into a room, do you brighten it or dim it? How do you think others would answer that about you? What are you telling the world that it doesn't know about you yet?

Are you happy, pleasant, positive, thoughtful, or kind? Think of a few people you know who are. In what ways do they brighten the room? What are some of their qualities you admire? They probably smile, act friendly, have something encouraging to say, offer to help, make eye contact, dress nicely. They have good energy. They are moving around and meeting everyone they can. They are confident. They are comfortable in their own skin.

Remember that everything matters.

Let's take a look at someone who dims the room. They are keeping to themselves more. They probably aren't smiling or reaching out to say hello to a stranger. Their greetings toward others are more subdued. Their energy level is way lower. They may be glued to their phone, so they don't have to make eye contact or talk to anyone. They probably find their seat quickly so they don't have to interact. They simply look like they would rather be somewhere else.

When I host a networking event, I ask the guests to stand up and do their 45-second commercial. You can learn a lot about someone by how they act while the others are speaking. Are they respectful and actively listening or are they distracted? The idea is to give everyone your full attention as they should you. You make others feel important with your attention.

I start with this observation about how people show up, because how you do anything is how you do everything.

You have a reputation right now. You may or may not like it, but you can change it. Awareness is always the first step. You may be more introverted and this may be uncomfortable, like it is for me. But the more that you do it, the easier it will become.

I want you to start with noticing how you show up and make an effort to make a great first impression. For the next week, make a conscious effort to brighten every room you walk in to.

Imagine if you were always the most positive person in the room. Do you think people would want to be around you more? Also make an effort to find the dimmers and help make them more comfortable. Make them smile or laugh. Introduce them around. Help them build their confidence.

Promptness Is a Choice

It says a lot about how you feel about the other person when you choose to be on time or choose to run late. That's right, it's a choice. In fact, it is a habit. We all deal with the same factors.

The person who will use traffic or some other outside influence as an excuse for being late will do the same thing when the big project or goal isn't met. The same person who plans ahead and arrives early will treat their goals and tasks the same way.

> "If you can't be on time, be early."
> – Harland Stonecipher

They think of everything. A person who calls to confirm an appointment values their time and values your time.

People are watching you. If you are constantly late, you are telling the world you do not have it together and you cannot be relied upon or trusted. Ouch.

Make a choice, starting right now, to be early and prepared for everything you do.

One Discipline Affects the Next

"If a guy is forty and broke, I would check his cholesterol," quirked Jim Rohn during his weekend seminar. Are you telling me one has to do with the other? Yes, it is called a clue.

Every discipline affects the next.

When you exercise regularly and take care of yourself, you are sending a message to the universe about how you feel about yourself. You are probably more likely to have goals and treat your career the same way. You probably put thought into your personal and financial life as well. It all works together.

Everything matters.

Have you ever helped someone move with five or six other people? There are always a few who are hustling, organized, and even helping the others carry some of their load. Then you have a few who are moving slower, and are even in the way.

It's the same thing in life. You are making things happen, watching things happen, or wondering what the hell just happened.

Day 29
Stay Inspired

We are all motivated by different things in different ways. I personally love getting motivated, inspired, pumped up, or as the kids are saying, "jacked."

I am a sucker for a good book, a good comeback story, or a life-changing weekend.

Change does take time, but it has to start. You can begin change today.

Imagine you were driving through the desert, and let's say you were headed toward the ocean. At some point, you decide to turn around and head back to the city.

Just because you changed your mind, has the scenery changed? Nope. You look outside and you still see sand and the occasional cactus. It still looks like a barren desert.

In fact, because of the momentum, you are still headed toward the beach, even though you decided to turn around. At some point, you slow the car down and stop, then head back to the city. Again, has what you see on the outside changed yet? Nope. You are still looking at dirt, tumbleweeds, and cacti.

You keep driving and driving, expecting to see different scenery, but it takes longer than you want. Even though, on the inside, you feel like you are making progress, on the outside everything appears to be the same.

It is a good thing there is a path with signs to follow, and maybe you even have a GPS or compass, or you would really be lost and confused.

This same thing happens on our path to a better, more fulfilled life. Some of us have been going the wrong way for quite some time. We may be suffering from the compounded effect of making simple or massive errors in judgment for years and years. That momentum has to be stopped, and we have to get momentum going in the other direction.

> "You can't change your destination overnight, but you can change direction overnight, and your direction will one day determine your destination."
> – Jim Rohn

Just because you have decided to change doesn't mean things will change immediately. You will probably be experiencing change on the inside. You are more excited about life. There may be a new bounce to your step. You can see where you are going, but others may not. Change can happen with a snap of the finger, but results will take longer. It takes time to develop new habits and see the kind of results you want. Be patient.

Have you ever driven by a construction site and it looks like the workers are just standing around, because you can't see any progress? Month after month, you drive by and you might even mumble, "Jeesh, what are these guys doing? They must be getting paid by the hour."

Then one day, the entire building is up, and you are commenting, "Whoa, that was fast. It seems like just yesterday when nothing was happening."

Change on the inside is hard to see. It takes time to build a foundation or infrastructure. A solid foundation will be worth it, though.

I call that feeling on the inside no one can see "inspiration." You can't see it, but you can feel it. When you are inspired, you are vibrating on a different level. You are telling the world, watch out! I have some big plans and I am going to make them happen.

It will take 3-5 years to be successful or the rest of your life to fail. With our family business, for the first four years, you could have looked in from the outside and thought, "These guys are wasting their time, where are the results?"

We were still living with our sister. We were still driving a beat-up Geo Metro. We were scraping by financially. Our incomes didn't drastically change overnight. Our relatives and friends were still making fun of us, more than ever.

But like I have discussed throughout the book, we were learning and applying all of the 30 ways consistently, with the right attitude.

Before too long, people started saying, "Wow, those guys came out of nowhere." Our reputation today is that we have been succeeding for a long time, with a super solid foundation built on all the principles I have shared so far. Now some call us lucky, because most of the people around today didn't even know us when we were struggling.

What Inspires You?

When I need to be productive, I get in a zone. When are you in your zone? When I write, I need to be alone with no distractions. For me, it is early in the morning, before the commotion of the day begins.

When I am prospecting or need to make important calls, I need to stand up and get my energy going. Motion creates emotion. I pace. I pace all over the house.

If I am going to speak to an audience, I like to have music playing so the energy of the crowd is right. I may sneak off to find a mirror and declare, "I like myself and I love my work." If it is a really big talk, I'll visualize my late parents smiling and telling me they are proud of me.

You have to find what motivates you and do that. Once you are in that state, do your highest payoff activity possible. Live in that zone and take inspired action.

When I am writing a book, I write for two hours in the morning. I don't walk the dog or have breakfast. I don't check my Facebook or look at my phone. I need every ounce of energy and focus.

When I'm finished, I am often exhausted.

I feel the same way after I do a seminar on a Saturday. Typically, I will speak for four straight hours. When I'm finished, I'm tired. When you are in a zone, it is like your energy is on turbocharge. Get inspired and then take inspired action.

I strongly suggest getting away from the craziness of the world every day, for at least a few minutes, and be with your own thoughts. Whether it is meditating, yoga, long walks, or going to the gym with your headset with your favorite jam, get away every day and just be.

DAY 30

The Day of Disgust
With Mike Melia

We have spent the last 30 days together sharing ideas about how to live a better life, accomplish our goals, and eventually live our dreams.

On average, we all live 28,000 days. I hope you use the last 30 days as an investment into however many you have left. Of all the days, though, there are a few that will make all of the difference. These are the days that turn your life around.

A man was walking by a house in his neighborhood when he noticed a dog on the front porch howling repeatedly. He finally walked up to the old-timer sitting on his rocking chair and yelled, "Is your dog ok? He seems to be whining."

"He's fine. He's just lying on a nail."

"On a nail? My goodness, why doesn't he just get up and move?"

"I guess it doesn't hurt that bad yet."

Ouch! How many of us are like that poor, howling dog? We know we are in pain, but it just doesn't hurt that badly yet?

Jim Rohn often recalls the story of the Girl Scout who knocked on his door many years ago, selling cookies. The cookies were $2 and he didn't have it.

"Sorry, we bought at the office and have a lot of boxes stacked up inside," he said, which was a lie. The girl politely thanked him and went along. As Jim closed the door, he thought, lie to a girl scout, how much lower can you get?

He resolved to never be in that situation again.

My Days of Disgust – with Mike Melia

Most of us have learned to settle for less than is available in life. It is a compounded result from "negative" conditioning.

These words from my brother, Mike, are powerful and incredibly deep:

> There is often an underlying feeling or even a conscious knowledge that we are capable of achieving much more than we are. For many of us, there is a dramatic moment that leads to a powerful decision to do better in life – hence, "the day you turn your life around."

> Back in the early 90's, a couple of weeks before Christmas, I was living in New York City. I was pretty much just getting by. I had some plans and such and I was working on them, but still I was just getting by, and I mean just barely.

My dad, a retired FDNY battalion chief, lived down in Sebastian, Florida. He gave me a phone call and told me he was going in for heart surgery the following week. My six brothers and sisters all made plans to go and be there for him. I couldn't afford it. I didn't have enough money for a plane ticket.

I was 42 years old. I wasn't so much ashamed as I was angry with myself. How had I engineered this level of financial failure after all of these years on the planet? I knew there was nobody to blame but myself. It was a day of disgust. My disgust went deep. At that moment, an inner desire was ignited. It burned hot.

I can only describe my experience at that moment, and it is still somewhat of a mysterious event to me. On that day, in that moment of disgust, I resolved to change my life's predominant circumstances. I resolved to create a level of success beyond what I had known up until that point – far beyond.

I resolved to find a way to change my financial fortunes. I didn't know how I was going to do that, but it did not matter. The resolution gave birth to a burning desire within me to create a massive change.

For some of us, that one day of disgust is all it takes. Yet, more often, that first day of disgust is reinforced by further days of disgust.

I resolved to make that change in December, but by the following August, there was not much visible change in my circumstances.

That August, my oldest child, my son Luke, was going off to college. His tuition was $21,000 for that first year. The cost of top-rated universities continued to escalate year after year. I knew, given my current resources, I could not contribute to his educational expenses, not to mention his three younger siblings.

This reinforced the resolution I made on that first Day of Disgust.

I share this because I know many people have experienced a day of disgust, but still feel lost in the wilderness.

I say to you, continue your daily practice of writing down your goals and expressing gratitude, and acknowledging your successes, even if they seem insignificant at this juncture.

Those days of disgust eventually led to days of freedom. I was able to say enough is enough, I don't want to live like this anymore. The change started with me.

May these words move you to take action.

Enough Is Enough

My longest job I've had after college lasted just about 6 months. I worked for a crazy woman named Ellen. Ellen was the first person I knew on Prozac and she never seemed to have it balanced out very well. One day, she would be as nice as pie, and the next, she would be screaming uncontrollably at her small staff.

Although it was painful at the time, she helped me have my day of disgust. I was taking home about $300 weekly as the entry level gopher, and I did any menial task she demanded, such as walk her two poodles several times per day.

It was a brisk Friday afternoon in early March of 1994. Ellen berated me in front of several of my co-workers for opening her mail, which was in my job description. I stood up for myself and she didn't react well. She threw me out of the office, and as I began to leave, demanded I don't turn my back to her and come back.

Once my decision to go was made, I was out of there. I can still feel the rage and embarrassment that filled my body as I fumbled for my coat.

When I stepped outside into the busy streets of New York City, I turned around and noticed the loud latching of the door. I looked back at the door one last time and silently pledged to myself that no one would ever treat me that way again. Never would I put myself in a situation where someone else would have so much control over my self-esteem. I would never be under someone's thumb again. I resolved that day to go into business for myself and never have another boss. Thank God for Ellen. I'm glad that happened at 23 and not 53.

Another day of disgust came at a time when I was 17 or so. I was camping with my older brother Tommy, his wife Lucy, and their two young sons, Timmy and Shane. I came back from the general store with two large bags of ice.

"I got 'em for free," I announced excitedly.

When Tommy understood I had really stolen them, he insisted I go back and pay for them.

He explained, "I'm trying to teach my boys the value of hard work, money, and most importantly, being honest. I'm not teaching them to steal."

Those words hit me like a ton of bricks. He cared enough to take a stand.

That was another defining moment.

I remember having one of my last cigarettes at age 29. I had just given a seminar earlier in the day and stepped outside of a southern California bar to light up. One of my buddies and seminar promoters, Dave, walked to meet me outside. One of my topics that day had been the slight edge.

"So, where does smoking fall into the slight edge? I hear you sharing all of these great ideas and here you are outside, smoking a cigarette," he said with a patronizing smile.

I knew he was right and I was being a hypocrite. Having him put it right in my face stung, but the truth often can. That night was my last night as a smoker. My two pack a day, 10-year habit had come to an end. Another day of disgust.

Hitting a low point, or even the bottom, can be the best thing, because you can rebound strongly. In fact, there is only one way to go.

Whether it is procrastinating, smoking, making excuses, or whatever is continuing to lead you down the wrong path, decide that enough is enough. Resolve to be disgusted and change.

The change begins with you.

You got this.

The change begins with you.

Afterword – Money Mindset
By Brian Carruthers

This book is brilliantly written to help us condition ourselves for winning by creating success habits. I encourage you to do the exercises in *30 Ways in 30 Days* until they become habits. If you have to think about and decide on your daily actions, then they are not yet habitual. Success doesn't come from what you do occasionally, but what you do consistently. By creating a routine – a formula for a successful, happy life – you remove the guesswork and put yourself on the automatic path to win.

Following these 30 ways will put you on the path to creating a better life. As you begin and continue to earn more money and build more assets, it is vital that you have a financial plan. As we all know, much of life's joy get stripped away when we encounter stress due to finances. Marriages suffer, children suffer, our self-esteem and confidence suffers, and we limit our options in life when we do not have our financial affairs in order.

This is why it is desperately important that we all must learn how to earn money, how to keep that money, and how to grow that money so that we can achieve financial freedom. I have seen far too many people derail their lives by making poor financial decisions. They let money rule their lives instead of learning how to be the master of money.

Recent studies show that more than half of all Baby Boomers will never be able to retire, I mean never. These people planned on retiring at age 65, but due to not planning effectively, they will never be able to stop working for money in their lifetime. This is a sad but true fact, and it is not something a person of any generation has to endure. You simply must make a decision to learn the proper money mindset.

Sadly through all of my schooling from private school through University, I was never exposed to real world financial education. This is why I set out to learn about money on my own, which became a lifelong passion. I wrote the book *Money Mindset* so that I could help people at any income level to establish clear goals and action steps toward financial freedom. For example, whether you make $20,000 a year or $200,000 a year, you should absolutely have a separate wealth building bank account and pay yourself first – 10% of every dollar you make – into it. This is one of the most important steps toward building your nest egg for retirement.

If you live and operate out of one bank account, you'll find it nearly impossible to get ahead because there will always be "important things" to spend that money on. There must be a defined plan on where your money is going before it's even earned. It needs to be spoken for, and you must stick to your plan. Focus on building wealth, and you will attract and keep it. Educate yourself and your family so that you know exactly what to do, and make it automatic so that it becomes like a machine that grows your net worth. I encourage you to pick up *Money Mindset* and learn the simple, yet powerful, action plan immediately.

Don't lose another day to spinning your wheels financially. Can you imagine how grateful and happy you will feel when your bank account is growing year after year? Get your copy of *Money Mindset* at www.moneymindsetbook.com

About the Author

Steve Melia is an author, comedian, network marketer, philanthropist, and a world-record breaking baseball fanatic.

Steve attended all 162 NY Yankee games in 2011 and wrote his first book, *162 The Almost Epic Journey of a Yankees Superfan* (2013). His second book, *The Last 42*, chronicles the final playing days of Yankee legend Mariano Rivera, while memorializing his brother, Jim Melia (2016).

Steve is a highly sought after inspirational speaker who focuses on the power of goal-setting, while using humor to relate to his audiences. In 2016, Steve launched The 162 Experience, a podcast about success in business, sports, and life with a goal to inspire viewers to live their dreams.

Steve, along with his partners, Mike Melia and Kim Melia, founded Work, Play, Love an organization that supports orphanages and children in Guatemala.

You can reach Steve at The162Crew.com or 760.522.5581.

Guest Authors

Kelsey Aida Roualdes: Kelsey wrote #ActuallyICan, a fresh blueprint for how to win at life. In this inspirational guidebook, Kelsey Aida shows you how to craft a new life that you love and includes hundreds of powerful affirmations to help you manifest financial freedom, radical self-love, vibrant health, kick-ass relationships, inner peace and more! You can follow her blog at: kelseyaida.com.

Kim Melia: Kim and Steve have been business partners for nearly two decades. Kim heads up their foundation Work, Play, Love and runs trips to Guatemala 3-4 times per year. She is a sought after success coach and teaches giving is living. To donate, volunteer or learn more, visit: giveorphanshope.org.

Mike Melia: Mike graduated from high school two days before Steve was born. The two have been business partners in their network marketing business since April of 1994. Mike travels North America sharing his story and encourages others to achieve financial freedom. Mike has four children and four grandchildren who continue to be his inspiration. You can reach Mike at: Meliafamily.com

Brian Carruthers: Brian and Steve have worked together and been friends for more than 20 years. Brian has surpassed $20 million in earnings and is a world-renowned expert in network marketing and wealth management. Brian is the author of *Making My First 10 Million*, *Building an Empire* and *Money Mindset*. To learn more Brian and his mentoring, visit: briancarruthers.com

Notes to Self

Notes to Self

Notes to Self

On Deck: The 162 HR Challenge

"Our Mission is to raise over $162,000 while inspiring others to live their dreams!"

On March 29, 2018 Steve Melia and Marybeth Longona set out to break Steve's world-record of 176 consecutive NY Yankee games.

Some predicted that the 2018 NY Yankees would break the all-time Home Run record of 264 in one season. So, they created The 162 HR Challenge with a goal to raise $162,000.

To make this adventure something much more than just what they alone are capable of, they teamed up with Work Play Love, The National Fallen Firefighters Foundation, Ed Randall's Fans for The Cure, and The Memorial Sloan Kettering Cancer Center to launch the #162hrchallenge.

The goal ... to raise awareness as well as money while highlighting these organizations on the podcast, The 162 Experience.

People pledge anywhere from $0.50 to $5 per home run that the Yankees hit, and 100% of the funds brought in are divided evenly between the four charities. (That's right, none of our expenses are being paid through these donations.) Every dollar is going to do so much good within each of these organizations.

You can follow our crazy adventure, make a donation or pledge at The162Crew.com

Play Ball!

— Steve Melia & Marybeth Longona

www.the162crew.com